ELUSIVE FAITH

ELUSIVE FAITH

Esther Seaton Dummer

DEFENDER
CRANE, MISSOURI

Elusive Faith
Defender
Crane, Missouri 65633
©2010 by Esther Dummer
All rights reserved. Published 2010.
Printed in the United States of America.
ISBN-10: 0984061185
ISBN-13: 9780984061181

A CIP catalog record of this book is available from the Library of Congress.

Cover illustration and design by Daniel Wright.

Scripture quoted is taken from the Authorized King James Version, with quotation marks added by the editor for clarity of reading and with deity pronouns capitalized.

Dedication

My book on faith is not about a person, but about a legacy of faith. For that reason I acknowledge four generations of my family line, starting with my parents…

To my parents, Delbert D. and Mary R. Seaton: sixty-five years of faithful sojourning. I am deeply appreciative to you for my heritage of faith! You have birthed in me a heart of faith in Christ alone—and the heart of a sojourner!

I love you deeply and have the utmost respect for you both!

To my husband, Loren L. Dummer: forty-two years of carrying on the legacy of sojourning.

I have been blessed to be by your side in this magnificent journey of the ever-unfolding walk of faith.

I love you deeply and look forward to the rest of the journey…

To my children, Donna Conley, Debra McBride, and Daniel Dummer: You were raised to serve the Lord with gladness and boldness—with faith and hope—with purity and faithfulness.

Carry on the legacy passed down to you.

I love you all and am proud to be called "Mom" by you.

To my fourteen grandchildren: You are the offspring of righteousness—young but fiercely faithful to your heritage! You are the fifth generation of our family lineage that has lived with unbroken faith in Jesus.

You may face things we have not faced, but faith is meant to endure. You have been prepared to finish your course.

Just keep your hands in the hands of Jesus Christ, your Lord and Savior and soon-coming King!

I believe in each of you!

Acknowledgments

Thank you, Jesus, for being my faithful Master in this journey of faith in writing this book. I acknowledge that this subject is too big for me, but am grateful for the anointing and for the wisdom, knowledge of the Word, and the Spirit of God working to direct my path. My only prayer is that I have not made it too simple or too complicated, but that it has met the mandate of Jesus for edifying and building up His church in faith for its journey!

Thank you, Gateway Worship Center! You have been prayer warriors of the most excellent kind, standing with me in intercession. You have been solid and sustaining—not saying much, but praying much. Who could ask for anything more?

Thank you all for believing I could do this! I am grateful to you all!

Contents

Prologue
    Everyone Has It 3
Introduction
    Keep the Main Thing the Main Thing 11

Part I
Prophetic Destiny

Chapter 1
    Prophetic Destination. 19

Chapter 2
    A Leap of Faith. 29

Chapter 3
    The Glory of the Impossible. 39

Chapter 4
    Don't Abort the Mission. 47

Part II
When I Say "Now"

Chapter 5
    How Long, Oh God?. 61

Chapter 6
    Sleepy Saints. 69

Chapter 7
    For a Time Yet to Come 75

Part III
Opposition? Count On It!

Chapter 8
    He Opposes You 83

Chapter 9
    Face the Storm 85

Chapter 10
    This Is Not Utopia! 89

Chapter 11
    Showdown 97

Part IV
Push, Press, and Pray!

Chapter 12
    Beachhead 109

Chapter 13
    Faithful, Frustrated, and Fallen 113

Chapter 14
    Holy Desperation 121

Chapter 15
    Appearances Can Be Deceiving 125

Chapter 16
    The Knot People 133

Part V
A Fresh Revelation of Christ

Chapter 17
    The Omega Christ 141

Chapter 18
    The Anchor of Our Faith 155

Chapter 19
    Invisible Faith, Elusive Faith 165

Chapter 20
    We Do Not Live by Sight 171

Part VI
The Keys

Key 1
    Believe God 177

Key 2
    Call It 181

Key 3
    Believe in Hope 187

Key 4
    Be Not Weak in Faith 191

Key 5
    Consider Not 197

KEY 6
Don't Stagger 201

KEY 7
Glorify God 205

KEY 8
Fully Persuaded 211

EPILOGUE
The Final Chapter Has Not Yet Been Written... 215

DECREE
Speak to Your Mountain! 225

About the Author 227

Carpe Diem: "Seize the Day"
This is a key moment—the day we open "the door."

Elusive Faith

Elusive: "Eluding clear perception or complete mental grasp; hard to express or define."

Faith: "Belief that does not rest on logical proof or material evidence."

prologue

Everyone Has It

F aith is a supernatural seed planted in a natural man by the creative hand of God: "For I say, through the grace given unto me, to every man that is among you, not to think of himself more highly than he ought to think; but to think soberly, according as God hath dealt to every man the measure of faith" (Romans 12:3).

During the last days I spent writing this book, I woke up one morning and heard the word "stretched." That word accurately describes me during the two weeks before my self-imposed deadline. In writing this book, I was stretched—not as in "this is a hard thing to do," but as in "this is never going to happen."

I have discovered a truth about myself: I am just like everyone else who has set out to do something for God in obedience to something He's called me to do. We get right up to the brink of completion after so much of the personal journey is done on a certain matter, we face the glorious moment when we cross over to the other side, and then we watch what happens.

Everything our minds and hell have the capacity for will throw us a fast ball laced with a curve to strike us out and stop us dead in our tracks. In addition, difficulties arise at the Jordan of our journey, and every problem that can arise jumps up to meet us head on, face to face, and we go into a serious tailspin of trying to keep our spiritual feet stable where we know we should be standing. The arm of flesh struggles to pin us to the ground in an illegal hold. This is a fierce wrestling match within our souls, a battle to the death. This moment, whether or not we understand it, is faith at its finest hour!

I am talking about a battle to break through our own flesh and thoughts in order to tap into the richest, purest, most vital vein of spiritual truth! There is a God in heaven who believes in you and me, and who is fiercely battling for us to finish our course with the banner of faith unfurled in His name—not in the name of any other, not even in our own names.

Your struggle may not be like mine, which is to write a book and have hellish stuff break loose against me. But you know your own battle with men, devils, and your own mind. You know the name of your Jordan, and you are acutely aware of the battle that ensues right at the moment I am speaking of.

No, it doesn't feel like faith to you, for you feel the title of "loser" being readied as an epitaph on the tomb marking the end of your journey.

I believe this last-days battle for the believer will center on where and in whom we place our faith, trust, and confidence. Thousands of offers are being made right now to steal your faith from you and place it in the arm of flesh—from raising doubts about who is going to pay your mortgage to questioning who's going to heal your body.

It's all about faith, and nothing else.

Let me take a moment to give you what God gave me on

February 10, 2010, as I woke up. The title of this book, *Elusive Faith*, describes the hard-to-capture nuances of something no one can fully understand in concrete form or come completely to terms with. I can't reach out and touch the part of me that was created and placed in me by the hand of God, the gift that solidifies my life with an inner strength to believe.

Without faith, there would be no victory or defeat. There would be no hopes, dreams, or aspirations. We would all stand as impotent beings who would not move out of the spots we were born in. We would be frozen in place. Our world would look far different than we can imagine, for faith is the core operating system of everything we are and do.

When a baby learns to walk, he or she must trust in the outstretched hands of parents urging, "Come on, baby, you can do this! Walk to Daddy!"

If you follow this train of thought, it will take you into every part of your life, from birth to the moment of reading this book.

Have you ever wanted to know what makes you tick, dream the dreams you dream, believe the way you do, and reach toward the outstretched hands of God the way you do? It's faith! Try to find one part of who you are or what you do that is not driven by faith, confidence, and trust.

Without faith, your talents would remain idle. Your dreams would be unfulfilled. In fact, you wouldn't even dream. The call to "go" would be met with lackluster eyes of nothingness because not even the arm of flesh can work without faith. You would lack confidence in anything of substance, because faith is the key to reaching out and taking hold of the things that create a purpose in life.

Without faith, the Bible would be a flat-line book of lifeless people with no stories to tell. If you took out faith, you would remove the people of the Word. Hebrews 11 would not exist. Acts 2:4 never would have happened. Israel never would have left Egypt. Gideon never would have gathered an army. Every story of faith in a common person working to the glory of God would disappear from the pages of the Bible.

Even the bad people of the Bible whose deeds are recorded for our understanding could speak nothing to us, for they, too, would have done nothing. The Bible is filled with stories of people who lived in the real time of their generations, who chose their paths according to what they believed and whether they put their confidence in their own arm or in God's.

Faith is woven into the fabric of our lives like the gears of a clock, and it moves the hands of time every day we live. Your day is faith-filled—settled on something you will put your confidence in.

Faith is in my spirit, my heart, my mind, my body.

Faith is in me!

Faith is in you!

I am created with faith as surely as God created me with eyes, ears, a mouth, a nose, hands, and feet—all that I am externally. As surely as my heart beats inside my body, faith works.

The Bible says that faith without works is dead (James 2:20, 26). You may not be doing anything for God, but faith works! It is coupled with works so as to be made manifest. Faith housed in us without an outlet is useless. Prayer and works are "faith with legs."

Faith works!

Faith is the God-given part of us that everyone possesses—just like God gave us His breath! The breath God gave us is misused by many people all the time to swear, gossip, spread rumors, give false prophecies, flatter, lie, and preach dead words to dead people; the breath of God is used by many others to speak words of life, preach truth to a lost and dying world, edify, and prophesy.

Faith misaligned and fixed with confidence on the wrong target leads kingdoms to ruin, elevates thrones above others' heads, rules with an iron fist over hapless souls, persecutes believers, and dominates as a world power. Atheists use faith—faith in their own minds that makes themselves God in His stead. Oh, they use faith. So do the cultists, witches, and satanists, who use faith to lead people along their paths of rebellion. Idolaters of the nations use faith, faith in that which "sees not, hears not, and cannot answer prayers" (Psalms 115:4–7, 135:15–17).

The last world leader will be abusing the faith God gave him as he elevates his head above the very God who created him.

While it may appear that those who exhibit faith in themselves are prospering, an end will come. Satan will fall from heaven. Kingdoms will crumble. Kings will die or go into exile. Wars will be lost. Nations will be shaken. Presidents will be voted in and voted out. Armies will lose. Best of all, the Antichrist will only reign as a god for a short while, and then Jesus Christ will dethrone him!

Faith connected to anything but God is a recipe for disaster.

With people all around us walking in faith along the paths of their own choosing, opting out of following God for pursuits of their own dreams and visions—yes, keyed by faith misaligned—God must have a people who will walk in faith *in His paths,* following Him to the ultimate end of faith: victory!

He gave us faith, and we have it and use it—mostly without a thought about what a precious gift it is. When trials and storms come our way, they buffet our faith and create frustration and anxiety. If faith weren't working, trials and storms would be useless, for they would have no shore upon which to beat.

We would simply stand there, losing nothing and gaining nothing.

You may say, "But I've lost my faith." It's impossible to lose faith! Faith becomes fixed on something or someone. You will have faith in what you believe—right or wrong. "Faith" is a God word, but it sometimes becomes fixed on ungodly things that don't deserve having faith attached to them—things that propel a person towards all kinds of ventures of the flesh.

But faith at work in a believer's life is an incredible thing. It's a high-power beam of light force that, released God-ward and fixed back on the Creator and bestower of our faith, does the things once thought impossible.

This faith will cast a mountain into the sea and march around Jericho. It will pray loved ones home to Jesus. Faith is the impetus behind intercession and the key to the release of the Spirit of God to work through our prayers. It connects us to God as believers, bringing us into a right relationship with the One who rewards faith.

My husband, Loren Dummer, said: "Faith is the hand of prayer that reaches into the realm of the Spirit, takes hold of the promises of God, and pulls them into the natural realm."

And in the book of Hebrews, we read: "But without faith it is impossible to please him: for he that cometh to God must believe that he is, and that he is a rewarder of them that diligently seek him" (11:6).

In faith, we will believe God's Word and tremble at the same. This faith will stand on the Rock, the Lord Jesus Christ, in the midst of storms. It will put the stone in the sling and hurl it towards the giant, knowing God is engineering the direction of its approach toward the giant's head. Faith moves us. Faith works in us and through us.

Look again at the keynote Scripture at the beginning of this opening word: "For I say, through the grace given unto me, to every man that is among you, not to think of himself more highly than he ought to think; but to think soberly, according as God hath dealt to every man the measure of faith" (Romans 12:3).

Faith is coupled with a call for us to resist thinking more highly of ourselves than we ought (not seeking our own interests or advantages), because once faith works to heal the sick, raise the dead, open blind eyes, and cast out devils, we are likely to take the glory from the God who put faith in us in order to work through us.

Faith without humility never could have brought down Goliath. Look at what David said:

> Then said David to the Philistine, "Thou comest to me with a sword, and with a spear, and with a shield: but I come to thee in the name of the LORD of hosts, the God of the armies of Israel, whom thou hast defied.
>
> "This day will the LORD deliver thee into mine hand; and I will smite thee, and take thine head from thee; and I will give the carcasses of the host of the Philistines this day unto the fowls of the air, and to the wild beasts of the earth; that all the earth may know that there is a God in Israel.
>
> "And all this assembly shall know that the LORD saveth not with sword and spear: for the battle is the LORD's, and he will give you into our hands."
>
> 1 SAMUEL 17:45–47

Saul had faith in his armor. David had a sling and stones, but placed no faith in them. Instead, he put his faith in the Lord who saved—but not with sword or spear. David faced Goliath in the name of the Lord of Hosts, the God of the armies of Israel. He wanted God to receive the glory and honor for what was about to happen, and he wanted all the people to know that there was a God in Israel. What faith and focused humility! David didn't waltz up to Goliath glibly; the young shepherd approached the giant soberly and in light of the majestic power of the God he served. He used what God had trained his hands to use, but he trusted God to direct those implements. We can do no less with what God places in our hands.

introduction

Keep the Main Thing the Main Thing

Because of what it cost Jesus Christ to open the door of salvation, I would be remiss if I talked about what we believe God *for* before I talk about the God we believe *in*.

Our faith in Jesus Christ is the foundation of every other belief we hold as true. If we lose confidence in Him because "He's not coming through for us," then our belief system becomes very shaky and may fail us unless we find solid ground in Jesus Christ upon which to stand and build our lives.

With the shakings coming to earth today, and with the scriptural promise that God is going to shake everything that can be shaken (Hebrews 12:25–29), it would be wise for all of us to find common ground with Jesus Christ, the only One who cannot be shaken in our lives.

Everything built on faith in and obedience to Jesus Christ has the word "unshakeable" stamped on it. So, it stands to reason that the flip side is also true: If anything is *not* established in Jesus, then the failure of that thing is ensured as well. The saying, "Don't get the cart before the horse," means someone has things all turned around. When the cart just sits there, people get upset because nothing seems to be happening, and they blame the horse because they are going nowhere.

There is a consequence to putting the wrong thing first when the whole movement depends on the main thing. Our relationship with Jesus is the main thing. Our salvation is the main thing. The movement of our carts is secondary, but they will move when the Lord is in the right place.

The first act of faith is belief in Jesus Christ as Savior, Redeemer, and Messiah! From that pours a relationship based on faith in Jesus' integrity, His Word, and His faithfulness in salvation.

From salvation forward, people make thousands of decisions that relate to their faith in Christ. They have many trials of faith when their faith stands on the chopping block of human thinking or opinion and is opposed by human and spiritual structures in place all around their lives.

Will my faith stand or fail? There are many enemies of faith, but a system of self works is one of the biggest. That system can set us right in the midst of a great move of God as a shifting of power from one hand to another takes place. First, God is in control—and then suddenly we "know how to do it."

Later in this book, I will be releasing some keys of faith, but in doing so, I do not want to mislead anyone into thinking that these keys are a set of things to do, like an eight-step pathway to faith. It's time to sober up in a religious world drunk with a continual imbibing of man's words and ways. We must take a long, hard look at the condition of the average believer—and yes, revivalist—today and the battle for the river that has ensued over techniques, terminology, and methodology. Many are more enamored with their own words than they are with the Word of God.

It is really easy to prophesy something, but it is another matter to have that thing tarry and linger just out of reach. It's important to remember that it is not what *we* say that is an active word; it's what *God* says!

It is not enough to make declarations and surge into the city streets to perform miracles. We are only complete and full of Jesus when we put Him first in our lives and take that message to the streets.

My cautious approach may seem to take the power-punch out of the subject of faith, but a good foundation couldn't be more important in this era of "easy-believism." Unfortunately, many believers look at faith as if it were something they have to do or say.

While I believe in the power of the spoken word, prophecy, declaration, and prayer, I also know that it is possible to beat the air with foundationless words and produce nothing that will receive a commendation such as, "Well done, good and faithful servant."

A great deal of talk, preparation, and ministry involves the "doing" part of faith, but possibly there is not nearly enough talk, preparation, and ministry that involves the "being" part of faith.

There is a very sobering Scripture we need to heed, one that leads all of us to the truth that relationship with Jesus is everything to Him—it is above all gifts, ministry carried out in His name, manifestations of power, and such:

> Not everyone that saith unto me, "Lord, Lord," shall enter into the kingdom of heaven; but he that doeth the will of my Father which is in heaven. Many will say to me in that day, "Lord, Lord, have we not prophesied in

thy name and in thy name have cast out devils and in thy name done many wonderful works?"...

And then will I profess unto them, "I never knew you: depart from me, ye that work iniquity."

MATTHEW 7:21–23

If we aren't careful, it is possible to do many things in Jesus' name and miss having a relationship with Him. Because we all want to be used by God in the way He intended His church to function, we can find ourselves circumventing the processes of God in our rush to the door to "take it to the streets."

To some this may sound as if I'm saying we shouldn't get out and go to work for Jesus until we get it all right. But that's not what I'm saying. I believe we need to get our hearts in a right relationship with Jesus to the point that He will declare, "I know you," before we try to perform deeds in His name. Jesus desires those who speak in His name to at least know Him. He wants to release the church that has been sitting idle for so long. The zeal with which many are ready to go and win the world is remarkable.

"Even so faith, if it hath not works, is dead, being alone.... For as the body without the spirit is dead, so faith without works is dead also" (James 2:17, 26). At no point is our faith perfected enough that we are granted a "work permit," but there is a point at which our faith in Christ and the relationship we have with Him validates that work permit for things to be done in His name! Even the smallest businesses on earth are concerned about who represents them to others. They want their images reflected in the lives, deeds, and words of the ones who work for them.

I encourage those with zeal to do their works of faith as long as the two sides of faith are active, meaning they aren't only producing fruit on the outside, but on the inside as well. Becoming like Jesus is the most important thing we can do.

Because of some teachings and prophecies given to people, there has been a very high expectation of performance of all that has been declared by the human mouth. Even when God has used a yielded vessel to speak a word or teach on faith, the way we take hold of it is of immediate and eternal importance.

Many times, people do not reach out and take hold of the Word or prophecy with faith, but with an emotional assent to what is being spoken. Christians spend much of their lives trying to "make things happen." This is a very frustrating expression of faith—one that places all the responsibility on *us* to "bring it to pass." That is the crux of the problem: People tend to look at faith as if it is always connected to making something happen. Then, when that "something" doesn't happen the way they expected, their faith wanes. It's not necessarily a disappearing faith, but a faith waning in a specific area.

We don't lose our salvation over these "glitches," but if allowed to stand without challenge, they can have a long-term impact on our faith in Jesus. The reason faith in God diminishes is we have connected it to an event rather than to Jesus Himself.

Part of the problem is our own timetable on which we want God to act. There is a kind of easy-believism connected more to *our* word than to God's Word.

Religious—and yes, even revival—trends and fads have always come and gone, but faith is not the latest religious or revival fad we take hold of and run with. We need to be careful not to be faddish people in a current-trend church world. When these fads and trends pass into oblivion (they will not endure) or merge into something else that challenges one's true faith in Christ alone, lives are left in shambles and rubble.

I don't know about you, but I have a whole lot more confidence in the things that do not change, fade, or emerge in a different form than I do in momentary excitement that so easily stirs, but doesn't change, people. Fads come and go, but faith endures!

The faith of many people has been decimated because those people take hold of an event, fad, or trend—even a revival movement—and make their faith all about that. This is very dangerous, and can have a deadly impact on the body of Christ.

Much confusion has been released into the lives of those who truly want to believe and trust God. As a result, many have had their faith shaken to the core. The faith of some has wavered; the faith of others has shipwrecked: "Holding faith, and a good conscience; which some having put away concerning faith have made shipwreck [stranded]" (1 Timothy 1:19).

Do you feel stranded on a sandbank of man's activity when all you want is to be a part of what God is doing? It's time to fix your course on a straight path back into the arms of Jesus and restore your relationship with Him.

He's been waiting for you.

Part I

Prophetic Destiny

"God has honored this generation as He has never honored a generation before. He has thrown dazzling opportunities before it. He has flung wide open for it the doors of access to all parts of His world and has laid at its feet every possible advantage and facility."

—J. Lovell Murray

chapter one

Prophetic Destination

Jesus Christ did not come out of a vacuum; He came forth from a well-laid plan that was drafted in heaven. His lineage was hand-picked by God generation after generation. The people God chose to be Jesus' progenitors were not some disconnected members of humanity; they were chosen to accomplish one thing: to bring Jesus to the world for the salvation of mankind. If we could drop into any scene of any of the lives of those listed in the genealogy of Jesus (see Matthew 1) and investigate what made them unique, we would find them to be people just like you and me. We would see them walking out their faith day by day, simply doing what were their tasks to do.

Yes, the lineage was human, but it was also a spiritually woven fabric of God's grace, mercy, and love that brought Christ to mankind. How did each "thread" of human life know his or her place and calling? God personally called each one out: "Abraham!" "Moses!" "Mary!" "You!" "Follow me where I lead you!" God has come to my door and yours and called our names.

Such an event occurred in our church a few years back. One Sunday morning in 1996, God stepped down onto a little plot of ground in a little town called Clatskanie, Oregon, into a little church building with the name First Assembly of God (now known as Gateway Worship Center) to visit a little group of people just doing what church people do—going to church. It was a busy church with all the usual activities associated with church life. People were doing what they did week after week: teaching classes, leading songs, and preaching sermons. On this day, we knew we were being intercepted by the One we served. His presence and our encounter with Him left an indelible mark on each of us. It was not unlike other times since creation that God had dealings with people. He began to move upon all of us in Gateway Worship Center, starting a pursuit of God that has continued unbroken for the past fourteen years. As we have followed God, He has continued to speak into our hearts from time to time to keep us aligned with His will and purpose, both individually and corporately.

One Sunday morning—on October 4, 2007, almost ten years later—Pastor Mark McBride, our music worship leader and a man greatly used by God to bring many people into a close encounter with His presence and holiness in worship, heard in his spirit the words: "Prophetic Destination."

As Pastor Mark spoke those words, all who were present felt the quickening of God's Spirit. With his words was a strong sense that God was confirming to all of us once again that He was taking us to a specific place. This was not some aimless, undirected journey of walking in circles; it was a step-by-step journey—one with a specific destination—engineered by the Spirit of God. Not only did this incident give us fresh vision to keep pursuing what He had spoken to us, but it renewed within each of us the thrill of the journey as well. I thank God that along the path He's called us to walk, He takes time to encourage us with a fresh word.

With this word from the Lord, we all refocused on the many

things that would culminate with God's plan being fulfilled in and through us.

What has God spoken to you about where He's taking you, or about His purpose, His mandate, and His call? Many people have received the prophetic voice of God through visions, dreams, revelation, and inspiration. The ways God speaks to His children, in part, reveal His plan. The way He communicates with us now is no different than the way He communicated with our forefathers of the Word or of past generations.

God speaks. And people do get a message from Him that is unique to their call and walk with Him, their ministry, their church, and their mission. Once we begin to pursue the plans of God, we find ourselves on a journey of such magnitude and requiring such perseverance that it can be somewhat overwhelming in its size and possibilities.

"Prophetic destination" speaks of the place to which God is bringing His servants, much like when He took the children of Israel from Egypt to Sinai and then to Canaan. There is truly a place in Him that He is bringing His people to so they may carry out His will upon the earth prior to His coming again.

Look at this definition (sometimes the dictionary preaches!):

Destination: The place designated as the end, as of a race or journey; the place to which a person or thing travels or is sent; the ultimate purpose for which something is created or intended; the purpose for which something is destined.

Folks, we have a destiny with Jesus! We have been created for this cause. We have come into the Kingdom of God for such a time as this. We are blessed to be a part of what God is doing over the face of the earth as He releases His glory! He has taken time to weave us into the beautiful tapestry of His work in this great hour. Too many times, we get so bogged down in all the negative that we miss the glory of the hour and of the fact that God has chosen us!

We are a people of prophetic destiny. God doesn't accidentally stumble onto a plan and hurriedly look for people who can enact it. He calls us by name. He knows our places, cities, families, histories, and backgrounds. He didn't make a mistake in calling you! He didn't say, "Oops, I really tripped up on this one."

He is a God of precision timing, precision works, and precision choices. Every building block He has chosen, He selected because of its quality and ability to fit into His purposes. God's plans precede us by eons. That is the mind of God: omniscient.

God is the most prophetic being ever, and He just happens to release part of what He knows to us. He identifies for us what He already knows to be true—existing—placed by Him.

God has it all in place, the position of heaven concerning anything He has shown you or released to you to do for Him. A vision is the precursor of something God wants to accomplish on earth for His glory. When He releases "the vision," when He releases *your* vision, He is bringing you into His plans—for a region, a church, a people, a family, a ministry…

God wants to partner with you. When Moses and the children of Israel came to the Red Sea, a wall of opposition was before them. If the story were just about a God who does miracles, the Red Sea would have been opened when the Israelites reached the water's edge. But instead, God used a man on a journey with Him to "stretch forth the rod in his hand" (Exodus 14:16).

Moses had been stirred in his heart while still in Egypt, as God had begun to reveal to him his true identity. Of course, Moses tried in his own strength to do the job—but he failed miserably. It wasn't until he came upon the burning bush—as he came face to face with God—that Moses came face to face with God's call for his life. At that moment, when God spoke to Moses, prophetic destination opened up to him (see Exodus 3).

It was the same with Abraham. From the moment God told him to get up, leave his homeland, and travel to a place of God's calling, prophetic destination began (Genesis 12:1). And from the time the angel of the Lord brought Mary the message that she was to carry the Christ Child and she responded with the words, "Be it unto me according to your word," prophetic destination began (Luke 1:31–38).

People throughout the ages have embarked upon journeys of faith that have had stunning finishes. Reaching the destination that God has called us to is an incredible thing. The journey of our faith in Christ as pilgrims on earth is an unfolding one replete with twists and turns, jolts and bumps, victories and human failure. But God has a way of urging His people forward. And then, along the way, an epiphany, an awakening, occurs—and we get hold of a vision that details a purpose unique to our journey.

The apostle Paul, previously known as Saul, was walking on a particular road in the opposite direction of Jesus—until He encountered Jesus. Paul's awakening released prophetic destiny in that moment as he was jolted out of his religion and thrust into faith in Christ.

My husband and I were talking about the vision, the Word, and prophetic destination when he said, "We are given the vision, but it is God who keeps the vision alive in us; it becomes a part of our spiritual DNA." Think about the words "spiritual DNA" and how powerful a vision infused into our very being is.

In speaking with our church congregation at Gateway, I reminded them: "The vision God has given this church cannot be cast aside. It is stuck to us like glue. Even when we have not understood what God is doing, we simply cannot put down the mandate the Lord has given us."

Similar things have happened to others, too. God has called out a people to Himself, just for His purposes. He signaled earth that heaven's plans were going to be enacted in some very specific ways. In the early years of revival, an abundance of messages detailed His promise, the call, the cost, and the direction in which God desires to take His people.

God didn't speak to just a few, select people; He opened the windows of heaven and sounded a blast of His glory and presence over the whole world several years ago. We called it "revival," and it came as surely as the "mighty rushing wind and tongues of fire" that descended upon the upper room and the twelve waiting on the Lord there.

And it came not in our timing, but in God's timing.

God has a long and effective history of redeeming mankind out of captivity—out of the messes His people have made of their faith—and setting them on a proper journey to where His fire burns. He knew what He was doing when He tackled this modern-day church in the hour in which we live.

He knew exactly what needed to be done to bring us to the "desired haven." He knew the path He would take us on. He knew the difficulties of that journey. He knew that all would not make it because the way would be hard and long. He knew that a remnant would arrive safely to the place He's taking them.

He knew they would be the ones who would rebuild the old waste places, restore the walls, and retrieve the holy things from the hands of the enemy and put them all back in the temple of God—personally and collectively. He took individuals and whole churches on the trip back home, back to the holy place where we would restore the sacrifices and serve God in obedience, with pure hands and clean hearts as His priests.

We are no different than our contemporaries of old who took the same journey we are taking now. Israel got somewhat testy with God, exhibiting impatience with Him and the leader God gave them. They simply did not understand where God was taking them.

He was not taking them to the Promised Land; He was bringing a people to Himself. The Promised Land would be where they would live.

We may make a lot of mistakes, move too quickly, and act without laying a good foundation. This is a human problem, but one God can deal with. Thankfully, because many have a good heart to serve God, He has been patient with us all.

Nothing with God is accidental, coincidental, ill-timed, or out of sequence. He does nothing in anxiety or haste. He doesn't put the cart before the horse and later regret not getting things in proper order. He never *reacts* to anything or anyone; rather, He *responds* to everything and everyone with a perfect mind and heart towards all involved.

Everything God does is exact, perfect, and right on time. He came at just the right moment to release something to His children on earth. Many were gasping for the breath of God. Like fish out of water, they were floundering on the shore, desiring the river of God to flow over their lives…and He came.

He came with a shout that could be heard around the world, and everywhere people responded. He came with a call for people to step out of the nominal church boat and trust Him for where He was going to take them. He came with a mandate for people to lay it all down and follow Him. And faith to believe God erupted in the hearts of multitudes from all walks of life, so they set out on the journey of newfound faith in Jesus.

The relationship with Him was restored with passion, hunger, and desire welling up in the hearts of men, women, boys, girls, and youth so in love with Jesus.

Prophecies began to be released.

Visions began to open the long-closed eyes of people who were now visionaries.

Dreams stirred people in the night watches as God spoke to man.

The Word of God came alive.

The Spirit of God began to move powerfully!

Jesus became real to people. Churches everywhere, people everywhere, dove into this powerful, prophetic, revelatory river of God and knew that He had spoken to them in such clear tones that there could be no misunderstanding. People, ministries, and churches all around the world began to step out in obedience to claim a piece of the territory as God gave visions of regions and people groups within those regions.

The lessons of the hour began to relate to Israel leaving Egypt to journey to the Promised Land. Mount Sinai spoke of "coming up higher" to a plain where God was. The crossings of rivers became prophetically alive with meaning as the journey ensued. The journey of Abraham and the claiming of new land spoke to people. The tent of meeting in the wilderness took on new meaning as we realized that we were also walking out a longer-than-we-thought, difficult journey of faith.

…And we had prophetic destination etched into our hearts, minds, and spirits so deeply that nothing could shake our resolve to reach the place where God was calling us.

…And we claimed our families, our cities, our churches, our friends, the harvest, and the nations for the Kingdom of God—all in an easy time.

But just because time has lapsed, the journey has taken a lot longer than we thought, and it has been filled with hardships we didn't count on, has prophetic destination been forfeited? NO! Like the character Christian in the book *Pilgrim's Progress*, some have taken wrong turns and ended up in what would seem to be a disaster, but Christian can always get back on the right road.

The road doesn't change or deviate. It is people, not God, who get off track! God has remained on course!

Some who are reading this may have taken a detour from the road. But God calls everyone back to Himself. It's as simple as this: Come back to the right road! The right road leads to prophetic destination.

Others maybe have not left the road, but they've become weary from the travel. The way has been long, hard, and demanding. Their minds have been taxed to the limit, but they know they're on the right road. If you fall into this category, it's time to encourage yourself in your faith and push ahead. The promises, the call, and the vision are still alive and well—it is we who struggle so.

Pursue Jesus…pursue His Word to you. It's still there, right where He spoke it to your heart.

chapter two

A Leap of Faith

God has intersected mankind at many points in the timeline of earth, as seen by history past and present. God released His Word to people and brought them right into the middle of a divine plan, one that would take the nominal Christians and set them on a pathway of prophetic destiny. These God-ordained, divine encounters changed:

- Cowards into warriors (Judges 6:12)
- Jailbirds into princes (Genesis 41:41)
- Princes into freedom fighters (Exodus 3:10)
- Slaves into queens (Esther 2:17)
- Old women (Luke 1:24) and a virgin (Luke 1:31) into mothers
- A murderer into an apostle (Acts 7:58 and Romans 1:1)
- Pew sitters into revivalists
- Preachers of all flavors into passionate forerunners
- Worship leaders into prophetic minstrels
- Teachers into heralders of truth
- Children and youth into firebrands
- Prayer meetings into places of travail
- Churches into lighthouses

These have changed history forever.

And God has changed you; you will never be the same again. Whether or not you finish the journey, you will always know that God called your name!

God has been the initiator coming to arrest man's attention, to draw it from what he was doing to what God desires of him, to agree with Him for something beyond man's strength or abilities. God meets man for purpose: The divine meeting the mortal has brought people right up to the precipice of human nothingness where God moves and man leaps in faith.

What a marvelous thing to have God choose you to walk this walk, the same as He did with Abraham and countless others whose lives are detailed in the Word of God and on the pages of Christian history.

And most of all, you are in the company of Jesus, who took the journey of His Father's will all the way to His prophetic end.

With the first step, man enters an arena where his mind can no longer figure things out—and that is just as it should be, for where would faith be needed if we could see it, handle it, control it, and taste it?

Ask all the forerunners of faith, those in the lineage of faith walkers, talkers, and doers; they will testify that what they did had no map, made little or no sense to those around them, and took them right to the brink of apparent failure at times. All they were given was the Word of God!

Here is my definition of faith: Stepping into thin air and believing God will lay the road under your feet.

"Faith" is running into thin air, and "enduring faith" is the ability to believe God will keep you from falling, lead you step by step, and provide all you need to sustain you, as you need it.

Elusive Faith

When you cannot see the road, it takes faith.

When God says, "Get up and start walking," it takes faith.

When you do not know the next step, it takes faith.

When the storm is blowing with great adversity, it takes faith.

When the enemy advances against you, it takes faith.

When your mind rises up with arguments, it takes faith.

Prophecies, visions, and visitations from God come into our world with a powerful display of God's Spirit, and we are momentarily awestruck. Then reality sets in, and we wonder, "What in the world was I doing and thinking in declaring this so loudly?"

Here is a definition of "enduring faith" (as compiled from the dictionary): "To carry through, despite hardships; sustaining and suffering without yielding, walking it out in great confidence in God's fidelity and faithfulness of His Word; moving with a belief that does not rest on logical proof or material evidence."

Sheer human will, although it's an incredible force of human nature, is helpless against the enduring opposition to Christ and His Kingdom. For all our strength, we can be reduced to a pile of rubble if we flex our own arms, for strength is not faith. Prophecy is not about making up *your* mind; it's about God, whose mind is already made up. By the time He's talked to you, opened the door of prophetic destiny, and started you forward, He already knows your name, how He is going to do it, and where He is taking you. By the time the vision came to you, the heavenly blueprint had been drawn up, signed, and sealed. I don't believe we really understand the great care God has taken in drafting us into an eternal plan for mankind. We must get a grasp of this, or we will think we just thought up this "insane idea" out of our own desires—or that it was a passionate, sympathetic response to a momentary stimulus.

No, God's desires overshadow us, implanting within our hearts something great and awesome that shakes our world off an old foundation of faithless living. Mary, the young virgin, had to believe her encounter with the holy and know that it was not a figment of her imagination.

We must go forward in confidence that God is leading us and knows where He's taking us. Our willpower to do what we make up our minds to do will only take us so far when it comes to the things of God. Stubbornness is not faith. Dogged determination is not faith. In fact, some people say things like, "Well, once I make up my mind to do it, it's the same as done," or "I'm just stubborn enough to do it!" Or they say, "I have the tenacity of a bulldog; I don't let go once I bite." The only problem with this attitude is that willpower is nothing more than works without faith.

The *only* way we can reach prophetic destination is by faith. Faith is the key to the journey. Faith is the key to prophetic destiny!

We must be submitted to the plan of God for our lives because our personalities, our strengths, and our decisiveness will not stand the test of time. A faith journey is so wearing and tearing on our emotions, mindsets, and bodies that by the time we have traveled very far, they are worn down to a nubbin. But faith will take us places—into depths of joy and suffering, in the midst of storms and calm seas—and it will endure.

Much of what we determine to do is bound to our minds, the part of us that does not like giving up without a fight. But there are things that require us to reach to a deeper part of our beings for the strength to endure when all is seemingly failing around us.

Without faith, many walk away in despair or hopelessness. Our self-determination is simply not enough to sustain us. The "carnal man" looks with the mind through the natural eyes at the spiritual. This will never work, for the carnal mind can never understand the things of the Spirit (see Romans 8:5–7). There are carnally minded people today within the religious world, and they have been one of the biggest roadblocks to allowing God to move wherever and however He wishes.

I wonder if God ever tires of hearing His people say "God would never do that" when He is working on their behalf to renew and stir their hearts afresh. All God is doing is filtered through people's thoughts and concepts about Him, how He works, how He moves, and what He will or will not do. Many people are trying to figure out God, as to whether what is going on is of Him.

It is a truth: Saul's armor makes sense, but a young boy with a slingshot makes no sense at all (1 Samuel 17:38–39).

It is a truth: A big army makes sense, but Gideon's army does not compute, as it was whittled down in numbers (Judges 7:4).

It is a truth: Putting all the best soldiers out in the front makes sense, but the ram's horn and a shout appear ridiculous and dangerous (Joshua 6:4–5).

But these events recorded in the Bible were of God's doing, and they gained a great victory for His people.

Many things people do while commissioned by God do not make sense to the carnal mind. Even people who are more than willing to obey shake their heads at times and ask, "Huh?"

While onlookers of this age are saying, "This does not make sense; this does not compute—you have it all wrong," there are witnesses who say, "You are right on course; keep going. You're going in the right direction." A race of enduring faith, an uninterrupted line of believers, has never died out. Hebrews 12:1 says, "Wherefore seeing we also are compassed about with so great a cloud of witnesses, let us lay aside every weight, and the sin which doth so easily beset us, and let us run with patience the race that is set before us." We are not going to catapult ourselves into success by any earthly standards of thought.

God has chosen people for His purposes for millennia, and we are just the ones who hold the baton in our hands now. We cannot separate our lives from the "past witnesses," as if that were them and now this is us. We are of their lineage, the lineage of Christ.

In the course of biblical history, many God-ordained events have stretched the human mind, spent the human strength, and silenced the human will.

- **Stretched the human mind**—"Lord, I don't know how this could be possible, but yes, I trust you."
- **Stretched the human strength**—"I don't know how I could possibly do this, but with the help of God, I'll do it."
- **Silenced the human will**—"My mind tells me this is going to require everything I have, but here goes, Lord!"

God chooses ordinary people who are willing, and then stretches them to fit into places where the fearful and unbelieving would never go—something beyond ordinary, into the supernatural realm of faith.

Those God has used includes kings, prophets, judges, and warriors—men and women of faith of low and high degrees, not excluding all the time of Christianity from the Acts church to today. This includes all the revivalists of more recent days who prayed and saw revivals and awakenings. Add to that the innumerable pioneer pastors who stepped onto difficult soil to plant churches as well as the moms and pops of faith, some who are seemingly insignificant by all human standards. These all have been people who stepped out from the norm and took a stand in a hard place, a peculiar place, to do what God called them to do.

These are not all sophisticated people or those looking to have their names recorded in the continuing history of the church. Many have been called out of obscurity, mostly unknown and invisible to the world.

If we ever believed at any time that we were highly spiritual beings, we have had to learn one thing above all things: We need God now, MORE than ever, because what He has asked us to do is virtually impossible without Him!

Incredible, Extraordinary, Impossible, Improbable, and Implausible

Zechariah 4:6 says, "Not by might, nor by power, but by my spirit, saith the LORD of hosts." We believe something so incredibly extraordinary that many people simply can't believe it, whether it's transformation in a certain area, the return of miracles to the church, the revival of a region, an awakening in our nation, or a wave of righteous youth to rise up in the power of God. The things God has asked mortal men and women to do have stretched them beyond bounds of human might, power, and strength!

This is going beyond the status quo into the supernatural realm of faith walking. It's going beyond the existing order of things, present customs, practices, and relationships we have relied on.

Incredible: So extraordinary (think about what God has

asked you to do) as to seem impossible; so implausible as to elicit disbelief.

Extraordinary: Beyond what is ordinary or usual; highly unusual, exceptional, or remarkable; rare, phenomenal, special.

To break the norm (a standard, model, or pattern) of church life is to agree with God to position and remain in a spiritual place for a supernatural event (though not to deliberately aggravate) that will challenge the present condition and existing order of things, even at times appearing as a challenge to the power structures in place.

Impossible: Not capable of being accomplished; totally unlikely.

Many things in the Bible were not naturally possible, but they were fully accomplished by God through a person who believed in and obeyed Him explicitly. While many unbelievers abound on the religious landscape, others are rising up in faith to believe that God wants them to walk into a realm of the unknown to accomplish the impossible.

Improbable: Having a probability too low to inspire belief; unlikely to be true or to happen; not likely to happen.

Yes, you've heard it from others: "That will never happen." The word for "doubt" (*distazo, Strong's* 1365) in the New Testament means "to waver in opinion." History is not only rich with people who obeyed God in the hard places and remained faithful to His call on their hearts, but is also full of accounts of those who wavered and doubted.

Implausible: Difficult to believe; not having the appearance of truth or credibility.

These adjectives that describe what God has asked us to do

are mental barriers to those who don't have faith to believe that: first, God said it; and second, He will do it according to His Word. There are people who, in spite of what their minds might struggle with and what others might say to refute what God has told them, will proceed, not looking back with any regrets for taking a leap of faith.

You will only stand in the incredible, extraordinary, impossible, improbable, and implausible places by enduring faith.

chapter three

The Glory of the Impossible

God loves to take ordinary people and put them in places where they are asked to do something out of the ordinary, impossible places where the glory of God can shine. Luke 18:27 says that "the things which are impossible with men are possible with God." This Scripture draws a line between God and man, making a difference between powers and abilities. It reveals a deficit in us that only God can make up.

"Without Him we can do nothing and without Him we will surely fail," the song declares. The things God asks us to do may look intimidating and overwhelming, stretching our faith, but if we could do them on our own, we wouldn't need God at all. When we begin to do things without God, the impossible plans of God can never be enacted because He will not give His glory to man.

He is the power behind the impossible connected to the heartbeat of faith of mere men and women of God. I am reminded of Sister Archie Poole, the woman who pioneered our church in Oregon. No, her husband's name was not Archie—*she* was Archie! She came into town, a little Pentecostal church planter, to open a new work. She met resistance that she described in meager terms in comparison to the reality of the wall of opposition she faced.

I asked her if it was hard. She replied, "Oh honey, I went through things I have never told a soul. But God was faithful."

It was 1948, and prejudice was alive and well. She was refused housing, a bank account, and help from real estate agents, and was told she could not buy her lumber at the yard. The townspeople said, "We don't want your kind here; we already have enough churches." She eventually found the place where our church sits today, just outside the city limits back in that day.

What God gave her was a big, old, rocky mountain—literally. It was not a prime building site; there was not a single piece of level ground on the property. The mountain ran down to an old highway.

What do you do when God gives you a mountain as a gift of His trust in you? You pray and you pray, and you lean heavily upon your faith in God's Word and fidelity to you.

The neighbors remember seeing her pull up in her car, get out, and stand facing her mountain. The little boy asked his mom, "What's Mrs. Poole doing?" His mother said she was praying that God would move the mountain, like in the Bible.

As Archie was standing in faith on the side of the road, prophesying that the mountain would be removed and cast into the sea, an event unfolded about sixty miles away in Vancouver, Washington. The Van Port flood came and devastated much of the region there and along the Columbia River, a shipping lane from the Pacific Ocean.

There comes a time when what you are doing is interrupted by God's knock at your door. Oh, the ones standing there may not look like God or sound like God; they might just be men on

Elusive Faith

a mission, directed by the Holy Spirit to your door. People like that were standing at Archie's door, speaking God's answers to her prayers. It was some men from the Army Corps of Engineers who appeared that day to ask if they could excavate her mountain. They said they needed rock to repair the dikes that had been destroyed by the flood.

Sometimes, God shocks our senses with His ways and His answers. He gives us something totally impossible and then uses someone for His glory in response to our faith!

Archie Poole was glad to oblige. When the Corps members finished their work on her mountain—called "Miracle Mountain" by some—she built the first little block church house, now encased within the walls of the church we currently pastor as a reminder of the foundation upon which we stand.

What we look at as an obstacle might be, in reality, a miracle waiting to happen in response to our faith. We may see the devil in it, as if the resistance were so big that it could overwhelm our faith, but God sees a "Miracle Mountain" standing there.

Moving that mountain is nothing to Him, and when it moves, people witness the glory of the impossible!

Sister Poole could not remove the mountain she faced. She had no physical strength, skills, or money to get the job done, and people stood in her way. So she spoke to her mountain because that was where God had told her to put the church. She stood in faith when there was nothing else but God and His Word to her.

This is where faith comes in, when nothing in us is of real value to God but our faith and obedience. We do not have to be special, gifted, charismatic, talented, or unique; we just need to hear God call our names and then answer, "Here I am; send me." We have to reckon ourselves unable to do anything without God.

We have to be utterly dependent on His voice and the next thing He says to us. And we have to be used to waiting on Him…

God will ask us to do things that are impossible with man, but with God, it's not just likely to happen—it's possible!

The nominal religious world will never know the glory of the impossible because doubt, fear, and resistance travel on the comfortable and safe paths of tradition, men's doctrines, and religious activity. But there are people whom God has called to stand facing their mountains. It's all about perspective! It all depends on where you stand when you look at a mountain. God wants us to know He's the God of every mountain He places in our path. We need to quit bemoaning the mountain and begin to praise God for the insurmountable. It is a reminder every time we face it: He's God and we're not!

There has never been a time in earth's history when God's people have not faced mountains, obstructions, or overwhelming hindrances. Many records throughout Scripture and into the current day testify of people who faced incredible odds. Incredibly, even though we all know the great power of God, we still seem to struggle with *our mountains,* the *obstacles* we personally face. Our eyes seem to always focus on the negative side of each challenge, even when we are trying to move in faith concerning the things of God.

And, does it really matter how the mountain got there or who put it in our way? It could be that the mountain is the enemy who has elevated his head above our promise.

Red Seas, Jerichos, Goliaths, enemy strongholds, religious strongholds, cultural strongholds, mindsets, enemies of the cross…some feel as if the hounds of hell are nipping at their feet. Israel felt that way! Our response to challenges so much of the time is a mirror image of the Israelites' reaction to seeing Pharaoh's army hot on their trail.

Listen to the voice of the enemy, your mountain, the thing that exalts itself against you and your God! "The enemy said, I will pursue, I will overtake, I will divide the spoil; my lust shall be satisfied upon them; I will draw my sword, my hand shall destroy them" (Exodus 15:9). All those "I wills" in there sound a whole lot like Lucifer on the day he fell from heaven, the day of his demise (see Isaiah 14:12–15). The prouder, the more arrogant, the more intimidating, the more fearful, the bigger the mountain, the surer it will fall!

God ended the days of Pharaoh's bluster against God and His people:

> Thy right hand, O Lord, is become glorious in power: thy right hand, O Lord, hath dashed in pieces the enemy. And in the greatness of thine excellency thou hast overthrown them that rose up against thee: thou sentest forth thy wrath, which consumed them as stubble. And with the blast of thy nostrils the waters were gathered together, the floods stood upright as an heap, and the depths were congealed in the heart of the sea.
>
> Exodus 15:6–8

God didn't call us to live on a level plain, but He did call us to level the playing field.

While we live in spiritually rocky mountains, places of roughness, steepness, and danger, we are not called to tolerate anything that stands in the way of the Kingdom of God—not in our lives or in the lives of others, nor in our city, state, nation, or world.

If there were no mountains to face, there would be no place for the supernatural power of God to hit the impossible. God's people looked at the Red Sea as their mountain, but God saw it as His people's victory march and song of deliverance. "Then sang Moses and the children of Israel this song unto the Lord" (Exodus 15:1–12).

Red Seas are necessary to release victory. There has to be a Red Sea for the enemy to drown. The Red Sea was a natural body of water getting ready to sing praises to God, the Creator of the seas. The Red Sea to God resounded with the glory of the impossible!

So, here you are, facing your mountains. Many people who have stood for any length of time in the current move of God, out of captivity into freedom in the Holy Ghost, understand the difficulty of this hour.

You have not really been battling with your faith, but with your mind. You have absolutely no difficulty trusting the power of God to do anything impossible. When you sing or declare His glory, power, and strength, you are totally convinced in that moment that He is well able to take down every mountain, destroy every adversity, and remove every obstacle. You have not doubted for one moment the power of God or His history of the miraculous, the signs and wonders of His power at work in times past and current. When you read or hear of the dead being raised, you have no doubt that He did it. When you hear of people being freed from satanic powers and burning their occult books and arts, you rejoice and know that it is true.

Someone has said, "Christ does not want nibblers of the possible, but grabbers of the impossible." I like that. God wants people who are moved by faith in the omnipotence, fidelity, and wisdom of the Almighty Savior who gave the command.

Is there a wall in our path? By our God we will leap over it! Are there lions and scorpions in our way? We will trample them under our feet! Does a mountain bar our progress? Children of God, press onward! Jeremiah 32:27 says, "I am the Lord, the God of all mankind. Is anything too hard for me?" For too long now, we have been looking at problems that are bigger than us as mountains, and they appear as mountains if we focus on them. The truth is, our problems are a speck of dust, and maybe even an illusion, but Jesus and His Kingdom are the mountain.

When you focus on the problem, God looks small.

When you focus on God, the problem looks small.

chapter four

Don't Abort the Mission

From the throne where the dawn of creation broke over the earth…to the manger…to the temple…to the river…to the wilderness…to the people…to the Garden of Gethsemane…to betrayal…to the cross…the tomb…and the resurrection!

Every step, every move, every place is planned and perfected by One who knew who He was and why He had come, never faltering or going backwards.

It was the mark of a Man with a mission!

Oh, to be so thoroughly captured by a call to a vision—and to complete the mission as Jesus did, willing to go all the way to the finish line: "Now is my soul troubled; and what shall I say? Father, save me from this hour: but for this cause came I unto this hour" (John 12:27).

Jesus was born to die, and every step He took was with heavenly vision intact. He never laid down that vision or forgot it; it was always propelling Him onward, His eyes fixed upon the cross. He did not lose focus, no matter what came His way. By the time He died on the cross, He had faced more difficulty, persecution, rejection, temptation, sorrow, and betrayal than anyone should face in the line of duty. But when we know why we are doing what we are doing, we will face anything to finish the course.

The Old Testament prophets had foretold Jesus' coming in great detail. His life was not a meandering trail of last-minute decisions, but had been planned in heaven before it arrived on earth. The arrival of Jesus in Bethlehem as a babe in a cattle manger sent tremors through the forces of evil as they recognized the prophetic destiny upon this child. To the undiscerning eye, this baby would appear to be a child of average birth caught up in the crush of the society in which He had been born. Jesus' parents did not stand out in the crowd; they were met with "no vacancy" signs until they came to the stable where Jesus was to be born.

The enemy kingdom had been basically undisturbed by any permanent solution to the sin of mankind, but here was the ONE who had been sent to crush its head. Satan seemed to have planned a grudge match for Jesus from the time that Jesus, with His Father, had seen Lucifer cast from heaven, falling into disgrace.

Soon the enemy, through jealous Herod, attempted to and completed the annihilation of an entire group of sons of Israel—all in an effort to get at the prophetic destiny upon this one Child.

And now here was Jesus, whose very existence was a constant irritant to the devil, stepping out of the Jordan River preparing to be released into the level of anointing that would split the sin and sickness of the world wide open, breaking bondages and chains from people, and setting them free. He was to make claims that would challenge the thinking of the religious order of His day, claims about why He had come.

A tracking network had followed every step Jesus made, from the time He was a small child to this time in history: out of the Jordan River and into the wilderness! It was evident that something was getting ready to transition into a higher level of ministry because of the anointing and favor of God that had just been placed upon Jesus' life and ministry. This is why it was imperative for Satan to try to stop Jesus Christ in His tracks, aborting the mission He had been sent to accomplish.

Why was the devil so diligent in coming to Jesus not once, not twice, but three times in the wilderness temptation? Because he knew that if Jesus left the wilderness, winning over all the temptations, and got through this difficult passage, He would go on to fulfill the call of God on His life.

The devil had no choice but to try to stop Him.

This is the devil's greatest fear concerning you: that you will go on to fulfill the call of God upon your life. The devil knew he didn't bring Jesus to this wilderness, no more than he had placed Adam and Eve in the Garden of Eden. All he could do was to try to take advantage of God's placement of His people in specific locations, using this time to attempt to do his evil work of deception and destruction to the children of God.

Satan wants to destroy the plan of God for your life; he has no choice but to try to stop you, too! The enemy will use any method available to trip you, turn you around, and cause you to fail (or at least feel like a failure). He may use a friend or person who has the power of position to influence or pressure you, thus making Satan the co-author of the plan to cause you to abort the mission.

Peter did that with Jesus not long before He was to go to the cross:

> From that time forth began Jesus to show unto His
> disciples, how that He must go unto Jerusalem, and
> suffer many things of the elders and chief priests and

scribes, and be killed, and be raised again the third day. Then Peter took Him, and began to rebuke Him, saying, "Be it far from thee, Lord: this shall not be unto Thee."

But He turned, and said unto Peter, "Get thee behind me, Satan: thou art an offence unto me: for thou savourest not the things that be of God, but those that be of men."

MATTHEW 16:21–23

Jesus was so focused on His call that He shut out every voice that tried to shift His gaze away from His Father's plan. Jesus was a by-the-book kind of Man, One who did not deviate from the plan. He had to keep Himself pure and prepared for the sacrifice that was to come, so He sacrificed long before that day ever arrived. He was set apart; to do anything that would cause an aborted mission would be unthinkable.

It would be safe to say that all those who are reading this message have probably had an encounter with the call of God on their lives in some capacity. Many readers may be wondering when this call will come to pass, and other readers may be wondering where the call went.

Some may have had one setback after another and are on the verge of believing they were mistaken in what they thought God had spoken into their hearts. If this describes you, may I suggest that this is the best time ever to allow the Holy Spirit to clarify your call and purify your heart of all doubt?

The wilderness times are good filters and sifting times; we come out of them with only what God has left for us to take. We need these cleansing times to help us understand some of our own issues, such as pride, motives, positions we value, and religion. It may be that God has even allowed this time of wilderness testing to bring some to a place of surrendering something He has been after for a long time.

God is serious about each of us, so much that we must believe everything He allows to come our way is to help grow us from infancy to adulthood as His children. We all have personal disciplines that are lacking in our lives; this may be a time to look closely at areas that need to be strengthened.

Maybe some appetites are out of control, or there might be some exaggerated ideas about ministry that have ballooned to prideful proportions. Some might be failing to honor God with pure worship. Our hunger, calling, and worship are always open to being tested by God since they all directly relate to Him.

Remember the three areas in which the enemy attacked Jesus: His hunger, His destiny, and His worship (Matthew 4:1–11). From the devil's point of view, the tests were intended to destroy those three significant parts of a most powerful call on Jesus' life. From God's point of view, the tests could be used to strengthen those three areas that would set the nail in a sure place for Jesus.

Every move the devil makes is to destroy the mission, to bring us to a place of defeat so severe we will not get back up to finish what God has called us to do. For Jesus, it was all about the cross and the salvation of mankind as well as the defeat of the enemy. For us today, it is still about the cross, the salvation of mankind, and the defeat of the enemy.

One of the hardest things to do is to keep the focus when everything appears to be out of focus, when our vision and our promises are blurred by situations that threaten to overshadow the light of our life. It is amazing how fast our world can appear bleak to us, even when we are right in the midst of believing God for great things.

Appearances can be deceiving. The high view of the kingdoms of the world and all their glory could look pretty tempting to someone who is not moving very quickly towards the promises and destiny of God. Even a rock may seem pretty tasty if someone can cause us to see it as bread and smell it as bread.

When you have been in a secluded place, a hard place, a high place in the temple can look pretty inviting. If the enemy can get you to take his bait, then the call of God is aborted.

We must understand this!

Everything hinges on how we understand what kind of offer it would take for us to get sidetracked from the path the Lord has put us on. If the devil tempted Jesus so severely, then we are not exempt. It is not by happenstance or fate, but by design that we are called and placed by God's hand in a certain spot. If we look back on our lives, we will see a series of events that have brought us to this exact time, place, and assignment. Many of us have said many times over that we felt the Spirit of God leading us to a place, where we generally arrived with great feelings of anticipation of how God was going to use us.

We have also found that being "there" positioned us to face some incredible odds that at times seemed insurmountable.

I want to take a small space to talk to a group of people who are in a hard place right now. This brief section may not be for everyone at this moment, but difficult times are a part of all of our lives and seem to cycle around every once in a while for all of us.

I believe some of God's servants feel invisible and insignificant, thinking others don't recognize the call of God upon their lives. Some who are reading this may have had many false starts in which they thought their ministries were really taking off, only to find that they fizzled out…or so they think.

Some people see others' prosperity or church growth and feel like they are "ugly stepchildren" to God because He seems to keep passing them by. If only we would all remember that we send tremors into the corridors of hell because of the Spirit of God that empowers us to be where we are—because we have pressed and pushed and prayed and persevered—in tough times when the "breakthrough" has not yet happened.

Many of you are now in a place that appears to be the end of the road. Some have heard the lonesome, echoing sound of the door of your church or denomination closing in your face. Others have wondered where your brothers and sisters are now that the lights have gone out and darkness has settled upon your head.

I know: This all sound so fatalistic. Oh, but for God, it is!

If your life matches anything Jesus went through as He obeyed His Father's call upon His life, then you are in the company of a "great cloud of witnesses"—the "faith walkers" (Hebrews 12:1). The truth is, the wilderness-walking times offer us great opportunity to believe God in the face of the enemy. But it does take a spiritual leap of faith to keep going forward when we just want to run back.

The mystery is this: Even though we feel so low, we're at the highest place of promotion when God trusts us enough to put us where He knows we will face incredible odds for survival if we don't keep our eyes on Him. This is not some game God is playing with us, as if we were pawns on His great board of life and ministry. It is a strategic move He makes: having us face off the enemy so we will never be deceived by his lies, even in the face of tragedy, loss, or difficulties.

Western believers, in particular, are not used to facing real persecution, such as being thrown into a lion's den or being beaten and cast into prison, but we do face the dark and sometimes severe times that test us seemingly beyond our emotional, physical, and spiritual limits.

We have been teaching that everything is "Father-filtered" and that we are "Spirit-led." This is a harmonious relationship that quite often brings us to a hard place solely for the purposes of God to be worked out in our lives. It is easy to quote others who are going through a hard time, a loss or pain, or a spiritually dry period by saying that "everything is Father-filtered," but we soon realize how confused and alone we can feel when it is our turn to go through those times.

I believe that right now there are pastors, whole churches, and individuals who are in this place, a wilderness where we feel as if all hell is breaking loose. Their finances have disappeared, their children have backslidden, their church members have walked away, and the glory of God seems to have dissipated. They may have lost someone or something very close, such as friends, mates, or property. Their church membership may have diminished almost to the bare bones, and they wonder how they will pull out of that dark place.

For others, sickness has struck and brought them low. They have been praying, and because the healing has not come as quickly as they had believed, they may be questioning the effectiveness of those prayers. It's not outright doubting God, but simply wondering where He is. Many are trying to believe for a miracle, but they find that up-close-and-personal faith is different from far-away faith.

Oh, how we can pray and believe, and work ourselves into an

intercessory sweat for others (and rightly so) whose pain and loss we cannot feel. We believe that God is going to come through for them, right now…and yet we stumble in our prayer life and faith when we have to determine for ourselves whether God really is interested in us.

The wilderness experience is a difficult passage for anyone walking through it. Yet we have One who went through a time such as this, and He has never forgotten how it feels to be alone with the devil cutting loose against you.

This time of pursuit has brought faithful people to their knees again and again, as they dared to believe that the promises that God made are attainable. You have to "know that you know, that you know, that you know"—lest anyone take your vision from you. You have to be steadfast and, be it man or devil, you have to cling fast to what God has breathed into your spirit.

Studying the path Jesus walked here on earth should teach us some truths about staying true to the mission. He said, "I have glorified thee on the earth: I have finished the work which thou gavest me to do" (John 17:4). The manger was not a great start, and the cross was not a glamorous end. Jesus also felt the difficulty of getting the ministry into the lives of many people for whom He had so much compassion. He wept over Jerusalem as some of you have wept over a church or a city that is rejecting you even though your heart longs deeply for their salvation.

I was not there to see how He felt when He was tired and lonesome for heaven's shores. This old earth must have looked pretty dirty to Him as he saw into the hearts and motives of the people who surrounded Him. He saw the sin, the pain, and the enemy's influence over lost souls, and He smelled the air fouled with demonic breath.

He might have looked at the task set before Him as a mountainous undertaking—after all, He was here to redeem the world. His time of prayer in the Garden of Gethsemane depicts the terrible weight of responsibility He carried with Him all the time. We must remember that when we are led "up" by the Spirit into a hard place, every wilderness journey does have an end! "Then the devil left Him, and, behold, angels came and ministered unto Him" (Matthew 4:11).

VICTORY!!!

I have a feeling that when Jesus walked out of that wilderness experience after meeting the devil head on, facing him off concerning His hunger, call, and worship, and the angels had ministered to Him, He must have felt His face turn like flint towards the fulfillment of His Father's will. There is something about the setting of a jaw, the squaring of the shoulders, and the stride one steps with when he or she has come out of a trial in victory! Anytime the devil leaves you, it's a good day!

A fresh breeze of favor must have been blowing into Jesus' life as He stepped out of that time to choose His disciples and begin to perform miracles, heal the sick, cleanse the lepers, raise the dead, feed the hungry, and cast out devils.

A multitude of people are probably wondering, "When Lord—how long?" They desire to see that level of breakthrough in their ministry and have God use them as He used His disciples. This move of God has raised our level of faith to believe Him for things that seem to have disappeared from the church. There's just something inside of us nagging and causing us to fanatically hold on to things that others are saying will not happen. We are certain God is moving to bring us into that place of destiny.

I really don't want to go back to anything I used to have because it cost me nothing. I had to believe for nothing, and nothing is what I got. I know God is going to bring you out of the "wilderness-walking time," and is about to release many into what you have prayed and travailed for—the vision God has given you.

But until then...

Maybe the wilderness will cleanse our motives, mature our faith, and make sure the vision comes the way God wants to bring it to pass.

Maybe this time will cleanse the mission of our own agendas and vision.

Maybe this time will ensure that we are pure enough to handle what God wants to do with our lives.

Maybe this time will toughen our soft skins and take the whine out of us.

Maybe this time will show us what we are made of—and what God wants us to be made of.

Maybe this time will cause us to know what faith is really all about: going for something we can't see.

Fulfill the mission! We, as servants of God have a mandate upon our lives as surely as Jesus did: "Even as my Father has sent me, so send I you" (John 20:21).

Part II

When I Say "Now!"

"When I had the vision, the angels didn't just go there—
maybe they had stood there for a thousand years—
there's a season that is coming they are
waiting for—for the will of God to be fulfilled."

—Loren Dummer, September 2007

chapter five

How Long, Oh God?

How long have the angels of the Lord been positioned over the area you have been praying for?

How long have they held the net to catch the harvest in their hands?

How long has the hand of God been poised over your city and church?

How long ago did God make up His mind to send revival to your region, your city, or your church?

How long has He known the names of the people He would use as instruments of His will?

How long ago did He decide the prophecies and the prophetic messengers He would use to open the door?

How long ago did He commission people to begin to pray His will over this region? Were you first, or are you down the lineage of prayer warriors who have carried the same burden you have had to see God move?

How long will it be before God says "now" to the hosts of angels currently positioned around any prophetic region?

You are no different from the people of yesteryear who were called to step out of their old lives into the new but difficult, unknown, and uncharted places in God. It all began with a hope and a dream placed in the promises and prophecies of the revival, and a renewed relationship and faith in Christ.

Something came alive in you: something more real than you could have imagined. You knew that you had made contact with the Living God!

Many people reached out with great expectation as thoughts of what God was saying were expressed in the voices of many people. The message of the hour came from your pulpits, from friends, evangelists, and the Internet. You searched it all out and stepped into the adventure of a lifetime. This promised to be the most exciting time of your whole Christian life.

And now here you are, asking yourself, "Why isn't it happening?"

Yes, you have prayed, fasted, and stood firm when others walked away, and yet… The visual evidence and manifestations people trusted in to validate God began to slow down, causing many to wonder where He had gone and when He would do what He said.

And for many, the questioning goes even further. "Why is all hell breaking loose against me, my body, my home, my job, my church, my ministry, my…?" People who have believed God for signs, wonders, and miracles, and who have believed Him for saving their families or for revival in their church, have felt the tension of a long, seemingly fruitless journey.

"And they journeyed…and the soul of the people was much discouraged because of the way" (Numbers 21:4). *Strong's Concordance* states that "was much discouraged" means "to be short, to be impatient, to be vexed, to be grieved," and that "because of the way" denotes "a way, a road, a distance, a journey."

How long, oh God!?

Are we asking or just moaning now?

Do we have faith or have we become impatient with God?

Are we at peace with God's timetable or are we vexed in our spirit?

Discouragement is a very strong emotional response to the absence of the thing we need or desire. When we wait and wait and wait, discouragement sets in because we are not seeing what we want to see or getting what we want to get.

Yes, we know it is God working, but "at least if He says He's going to do something, then He ought to do it and not keep us waiting," could be the interpretation of our discouragement.

The definition of "discouragement" is "to lose hope." One reason we want to know "how long" is because the things we have cared about and are praying for appear to be getting harder, and time seems to be running out.

We see the hardness of hearts, cities, lands, and people all around us.

We see that wickedness appears to be abounding on every hand.

We see the laws changing, threatening us with loss of freedoms.

We see our loved ones' hearts seemingly getting harder rather than softer.

We see our churches still cold and indifferent towards the things of God.

We, like others before us, seem pressed down by such oppressive figures and statistics.

We seem to drown more in the opposing facts than we are immersed in the power of God.

Look at some of the psalmist's questions and see if you see yourself in them:

Psalm 6:3: "My soul is also sore vexed: but thou, O Lord, how long?"

Psalm 13:1: "How long wilt thou forget me, O Lord? forever? How long wilt thou hide thy face from me?"

Psalm 13:2: "How long shall I take counsel in my soul, having sorrow in my heart daily? How long shall mine enemy be exalted over me?"

Psalm 35:17: "Lord, how long wilt thou look on? Rescue my soul from their destructions, my darling from the lions."

Psalm 90:13: "Return, O Lord, how long?"

Psalm 94:3: "Lord, how long shall the wicked, how long shall the wicked triumph?"

Psalm 94:4: "How long shall they utter and speak hard things? And all the workers of iniquity boast themselves?"

Even for all our praying, sometimes we almost despair that the answer is not forthcoming...

Habakkuk 1:2: "O Lord, how long shall I cry, and thou wilt not hear! Even cry out unto thee of violence, and thou wilt not save!"

Yes, we want to know "how long." It is a question that has been asked over and over. But do we know that God has questions of His own about "how long"? To put things in proper perspective, let's look at some of God's questions:

Numbers 14:11: "How long will this people provoke me? And how long will it be ere they believe me?"

Joshua 18:3: "How long are ye slack to go to possess the land?"

1 Kings 18:21: "How long halt ye between two opinions?"

Psalms 4:2: "How long will ye turn my glory into shame? How long will ye love vanity, and seek after leasing?"

Psalms 82:2: "How long will ye judge unjustly, and accept the persons of the wicked?"

Proverbs 1:22: "How long, ye simple ones, will ye love simplicity? And the scorners delight in their scorning, and fools hate knowledge?"

Proverbs 6:9: "How long wilt thou sleep, O sluggard? When wilt thou arise out of thy sleep?"

Jeremiah 4:14: "How long shall thy vain thoughts lodge within thee?"

Jeremiah 4:21–22: "How long shall I see the standard, and hear the sound of the trumpet?"

Jeremiah 23:26: "How long shall this be in the heart of the prophets that prophesy lies?"

Matthew 17:17: "Then Jesus answered and said, 'O faithless and perverse generation, how long shall I be with you? How long shall I suffer you?'"

Do you think *we've* been waiting on God? Well, how about how long *God* has been waiting on *us?*

He has been enduringly patient and longsuffering, watching us fall down and get back up, watching our faith fail and then rise, watching our shortcomings and the hundreds of times we've been to the altars to repent.

He has been longsuffering with us, and He's seen something to give Him hope: the times we've risen back up to fight another day, to worship, to pray, and to believe that this is actually going to happen, even if we can't figure it all out.

People become impatient with God, so they tend to birth Ishmaels. Abraham, for all his faith, did this. He had waited for the promise of a child for so long that he finally tried a little self-help. The result was a disaster.

Many people have taken a similar detour off the pathway God called them to walk. They push the envelope to hurry and get what God said they could have. God wants the "child of promise," Isaac, to be born, so wait! If God is to do what He has set out to do—"Isaac must be born"—detours are not a substitute good idea.

Don't get ahead of God, because you will never be able to carry out full-term prophetic destination on your own. Over and over, people have had to learn this lesson the hard way by trying to reach the end of the journey *without taking the journey*. There is just no easy way to travel apart from simply doing the miles. Prophetic destiny must be walked out a step at a time.

And unfortunately, along the way, a multitude of people appear to have successfully reached their goals in life. They look back at many who appear to be trudging along. Don't be fooled by those who are in the "fast lane." I have found that the one who passes everyone else on the road can be found at the next red light, where you catch up. For all the burning rubber and speeding, their progress might be just for show. Everyone on a journey on God's road will have to complete the same number of miles to finish the course. If the journey is ten miles long, then it will be ten miles long for everyone on the road who wishes to reach the end.

It is called life—life that God gives to all to do what He has called each person to do.

chapter six

Sleepy Saints

Waiting is fatiguing! I'm glad the human body and spirit are separate from one another, in that while my body may be tired, my spirit is strong and active. I may be physically dragging with fatigue or sickness, but my spirit is soaring high above, trusting God for the end of the journey.

Look at this definition of "exhausted": "To drain of strength or energy, wear out, or fatigue greatly, as a person." We will face many battles as we journey with the Lord, especially if we have entered a new field of endeavor and are breaking new ground. We are much like the children of Israel who were told to overthrow the inhabitants of the new land, a king at a time, until they totally possessed the land. When they entered that endeavor, God was with them, but the enemy strongholds fought back, fiercely defending their territories, cities, and thrones.

This is the nature of spiritual warfare that erupts once God calls us to go forth with courage to conquer new lands for Him. We will face obstacles, warfare, rivers, kings, armies, mindsets, strongholds, and structures of power that have been in place a long time.

All sojourners who have been called to do something according to God's instructions have faced circumstances and events that threaten to wear down their resolve, tear at their senses, wreak havoc with their emotions, stress their nerves, and attack their bodies. Yet…they have journeyed on. We can do no less.

I don't know many warriors on any front of the natural battles the military wages who arbitrarily decide to leave the front lines to take a nap right at the peak of battle. I have no doubt you are hopeful about the promises and still desire to see all God has said will come to pass. I am there with you. I, too, have had my days of impatient waiting and wondering—especially if it was something that affected me directly.

I am restless, desirous, and sleepy—all at once!

Now how can that be? My spirit man gnaws at me all the time for what God has said He will do on many, many fronts. The desire is still strong, but I find myself weary at times! The state of weariness will cause our passion for the journey and the vision to wane. It will cause us to lack joy in our everyday lives, and it will even affect our worship of God.

"And let us not be weary [to be utterly spiritless, to be wearied out, exhausted] in well doing: for in due season we shall reap, if we faint not" (Galatians 6:9). Remember the disciples, after they had walked and talked with Jesus for so long? It was coming close to the end of Jesus' time with them, and the transition was about to happen. He took some with Him into the Garden of Gethsemane and asked them to watch and pray. However, a spirit of slumber came over them, right at a strategic moment in the ministry Jesus was finishing.

> Then saith He unto them, "My soul is exceeding sorrowful, even unto death: tarry ye here, and watch

with me." And He came unto the disciples, and found them asleep, and saith unto Peter, "What, could ye not watch with me one hour?" And He came and found them asleep again: for their eyes were heavy.

Then cometh He to His disciples, and saith unto them, "Sleep on now, and take your rest: behold, the hour is at hand, and the Son of man is betrayed into the hands of sinners."

MATTHEW 26:38–46

Jesus can ask the most penetrating questions. He asked His three most trusted disciples, "Can you not watch with me one hour?" I believe the closer we get to transition, our propensity to grow weary increases—not just in the physical sense, but also in the spiritual.

Discouragement can lead to defeat.

I don't know if it's the devil or us, but people today are so tired! I have noticed an intense fatigue and sleepiness, even in the most dedicated prayer warriors. In some cases, it's as if a demonic sandman threw his poppy dust all over, and they just nod off. As people of God, we have to fight this! Yes, we need to spiritually rest at the right time, but we must stay spiritually awake at the right time, too.

It is not okay to fall asleep at the moment when Jesus needs us to be awake. He did not tell His disciples, "Oh, it's okay; I know you're tired…go ahead and get a little shut-eye." Instead, He woke them up two times, and then at last told them to go ahead and sleep on.

Wherefore He saith, "Awake thou that sleepest, and arise from the dead, and Christ shall give thee light. See then

that ye walk circumspectly, not as fools, but as wise,
Redeeming the time, because the days are evil."

Ephesians 5:14–16

Jesus explained why He wanted the disciples to stay awake and watch: temptation. I understand that the physical body's weariness can be just that, but we can also cave in and stop due to fatigue, discouragement, or a failure to understand the days in which we live. It is a time of great temptations and change. While our physical bodies may be weary, our spirits should be alive and well, filled with faith—for the hour is also upon us.

We are in some of the most serious days, with the devil beginning to pull out his big guns and aim them directly at the heart of the believer, the church. Jesus calls, now more than ever, "Stay awake! Stay awake spiritually." I cannot imagine us not being there for Jesus at this moment in history.

Awaken to worship.

Awaken to the battle.

Awaken to the hour.

Awaken to the harvest.

Awaken to the season.

We are in one of the most intense seasons of difficulties and shakings, and Jesus needs us sober, vigilant, alert, and ready at any given moment! We must not hear the words of Jesus declare to us, "Sleep on now, take your rest; behold the hour is at hand."

Our spirits are moving with a greater desire than ever to see the fulfillment of all God has promised. The time is close and we know it, but we also feel the growing resistance. The world is restless, mocking and persecuting Christians at an alarming and increasing rate. The church is restless, falling deeper into apathy and compromise, declaring that it is okay. The nations are restless, in revolt against each other as wars and anger increase. The elements are restless, earthquakes and storms erupting in greater and greater levels of intensity.

Overall, God's people have been patiently enduring for many years. But recently, restlessness seems to have invaded the spirits of all who have been contenders for revival, for breakthrough on many fronts, and for the harvest. God's people are anxious to see the promises come true, to see the visions fulfilled—to see the "child of promise" born.

We need to awaken in this hour to increased intercession, increased desire to be where God sits us down for any particular moment in our history. The restless desperation in our hearts should remind us that we can do absolutely nothing without God, and it should bring a great cry from our depths into the ears of God.

Nothing is wrong with groaning (having no words to describe what you are feeling). But it's important to release the sound in the right way, not as impatient complaints and murmurings against the way things are or how long something is taking.

> For we know that the whole creation [sum of things created] groans [groans together] and travails in pain together [to undergo agony like a woman in childbirth] until now.
>
> And not only they, but ourselves also, which have the first fruits of the Spirit, even we ourselves groan [pray inaudibly, with grief] within ourselves, waiting for the adoption, to wit, the redemption of our body....
>
> Likewise the Spirit also helps our infirmities: for we

know not what we should pray for as we ought: but the Spirit itself makes intercession [to intercede in behalf of] for us with groanings which cannot be uttered [not expressed in words].

ROMANS 8:22–23, 26

There are things we desire so deeply that they have long ago ceased being the subject of intelligent prayer. We don't even know what to say any more on the subject. We are exhausted and have exhausted our tomes of words. That's good, because we know how to pray our minds. It's a good thing to come to the end of ourselves.

I believe the groaning, inaudible sounds of the spirit man crying out with the heart finally broken over the same things God's heart is broken over, at this stage, are a deeper intercession than anything to wit. It is a last-stage labor, a travail that leads to the birth of the promise.

chapter seven

For a Time Yet to Come

Recently, the Holy Spirit quickened my spirit. I turned to the book of the Revelation of Christ, as I felt directed, to the greatest prophetic vision and book ever. John, the one who received the visitation and saw the visions, never saw the fulfillment of the revelation he was given.

What he heard and saw was written in this prophetic book for a time yet to come. While this prophecy is yet to be fulfilled, it also reveals the continuing way God works. It is a prophetically profound book illustrating how God moves, His preparation, His readiness, and the people He uses.

There is a pattern of release. That pattern contains key components.

We see John, the visionary; his encounter with Jesus; the vision of what is to come; revelation concerning the church and Jesus' issues with their condition; God's throne; the worship that is taking place around everything God does; and the prayers of the saints. We also see Jesus seated and worthy. We find the angels are very much a part of the release of the prophetic decree. We see all the key implements used by God, the plan, released from His heavenly drawing board centuries ago to be released in "a time yet to come."

> And he said unto me, "These sayings are faithful and true: and the Lord God of the holy prophets sent His angel to show unto His servants the things which must shortly be done. Behold, I come quickly: blessed is he that keeps the sayings of the prophecy of this book."
>
> Revelation 22:6–7

The words spoken by Jesus, "These sayings are faithful and true," released faith in the promise of things to come. When Jesus used the words, "that must shortly be done," John may have thought the events would take place in his lifetime. But prophecy has, for the most part, an "incubation period" during which the Holy Spirit broods over it while God's people nurture it in their hearts—until it comes to pass. It is a "let Your will be done on earth as it is in heaven" moment.

The Revelation of Jesus Christ to John is a powerful book revealing how God starts and finishes things—complete, detailed, precise, and specific—and how prepared He and everyone around Him are in executing His plan to the final detail.

Well, God has started and finished a lot of things throughout the millennia, including two Great Awakenings. He started and finished preparing Israel, down to every detail, including each and every border and who would inhabit each area—her beginning and her final state. He named the winners and losers of the battles past, and He already has named the last-days winners and losers.

When God has set His mind to accomplish a matter, it is done when it leaves His mouth. He performs all He speaks. His Word will not, does not, and cannot return to Him void (barren): "For as the rain cometh down, and the snow from heaven, and returns not thither, but waters the earth, and makes it bring forth and bud, that it may give seed to the sower, and bread to the eater" (Isaiah 55:10). Note the parallel drawn between rain and God's Word. Just as the rain and snow fall on earth to water it, so God's Word falls on earth. God waters the earth with His Word. From that Word, a bud forms for two reasons: seed and food. Seed is given to the sower and bread to the eater.

"So shall my word be that goes forth out of my mouth: it shall not return unto me void [it shall not be without cause, empty, or of no effect], but it shall accomplish that which I please, and it shall prosper in the thing whereto I sent it" (Isaiah 55:11). God's Word is not barren. It's not sent without a cause, and when it is sent, it is not vain or empty, but a live seed. This should fill us with great faith over the prophecies, visions, and revelations we have received in our era.

God has prophesied revival, awakening, salvation, healing, and deliverance to your life, region, family, or church, just as He has for the world. He has spoken this to us, His servants here and in the lands beyond. Sometimes we are prone to believe in, pray for, press into, and war for the cause, and we lose sight of Jesus in all the scurrying around to do the work and will of God. We need to remember that there is no beginning or end, no alpha or omega, no first or last without Jesus: "Looking unto Jesus, the author and finisher of our faith" (Hebrews 12:2a). We need to keep our eyes on the Author and Finisher of our faith.

John records the reason for Jesus' appearance: "To show His servants things which must shortly come to pass" (Revelation 1:1).

What has the Lord told you?

What has He shown you?

What has He promised?

What have you been carrying in your prayer journal for so long?

I don't believe I have ever heard of a forerunner living the proverbial "life of Riley," but I have heard multiple stories of trials of faith as people pursued God's call on their lives. Look at the early disciples, the revivalists, the missionaries, and other ground-breaking ministries of countless numbers who have gone on before us.

John was no different. When Jesus came to him, He was in a place quite similar to the location of some of God's people today. He was in a hard place. His hard race had landed him in a hard place—and all for refusing to give up his faith! Now that's some payday for staying faithful to God's claim upon his life...or so one would think. But think again: "I, John, who also am your brother, and companion in tribulation, and in the kingdom and patience of Jesus Christ, was in the isle that is called Patmos, for the word of God, and for the testimony of Jesus Christ" (Revelation 1:9).

John is saying, "I was physically in a place of imprisonment, a place that was personally very restrictive and difficult." He had been faithful to preach the Word and give testimony of Jesus Christ. He had not been ashamed to stand up for Jesus, and he now found himself in this island prison among the guilty and wicked men sent there to die.

Everyone who has contended for any length of time started with a great passion and tremendous hope and zeal for what God said He would do. But they have now found that they are in a place that has stretched them emotionally, mentally, physically, and spiritually.

I hear it from people all over—those who have received powerful promises of revival, healing, salvation, and deliverance—who are now in a hard place, in their own Patmos, as it were.

Many have been limited by their circumstances (in a hard place)…but at times they have used that difficulty as an excuse for why they can't seem to "get into worship," "seek Jesus," or "be faithful to serve God."

John was not spiritually limited by his circumstances.

It was in the hardest and most isolated place of great limitations and difficulties that he was mightily visited by Jesus. John had learned a secret we must all learn—to worship the One who is worthy—in a hard place, under the most adverse of circumstances.

John entered a place in the Spirit that took him away from the reality of the hard ground, the prison walls, the scars of persecution, the isolation, and the hardships he suffered. He said, "I was in the Spirit on the Lord's day, and heard behind me a great voice, as of a trumpet" (Revelation 1:10). Are you discouraged with your circumstances and the length of time it is taking? Get in the Spirit! The Lord's Day is any day you want to make it. When you are in the presence of God, time no longer really matters; you just want to be where He is. And in that place, He will encourage you and speak to you. God loves to meet us at ground zero, in places we never would think God would show up.

Part III

Opposition? Count On It!

"But thanks be to God, which gives us the victory through our Lord Jesus Christ. Therefore, my beloved brethren, be ye steadfast, unmovable, always abounding in the work of the Lord, forasmuch as ye know that your labor is not in vain in the Lord."

1 CORINTHIANS 15:57–58

chapter eight

He Opposes You

Let's just come and right out and define our enemy by name: the devil. He hates you. He hates God's Word to you and in you. He hates the promises. He hates true prophecy. He hates worship of God. He hates God, and He hates you.

He has no benevolence in him. He is utterly dark, filled with unspeakable atrocities and wretchedness. He has the title of "liar" (John 8:44). He has the job description of "steal, kill, and destroy" (John 10:10). He does his work in darkness; not an ounce of light is in him. He is sneaky, stealthy, undermining, and manipulative.

He offers the world and takes the soul (Matthew 4:8–9).

He is the enemy. He goes about as a roaring lion seeking whom he may devour (1 Peter 5:8). His appetite is insatiable; his belly is never filled. His cravings for deeper and darker depravity cause him to go to depths of evil that bring ruin to humanity.

He is the engineer of child sacrifice, abortion, and abuse. He is the architect of rape, murder, ethnic cleansing, and genocide—any kind of killing. He is the drafter of evil pacts and hellish agreements made to bind mankind to himself in bloody rituals and crafts. He is the manufacturer of gossip, slander, lies, false accusation, false prophecies, splits in human relationships, divorce, and every other divisive thing. He is the mastermind of rebellion, stubbornness, and pride. And he is the opposing force against everything God plans to do through you.

He hears the prophecy, he sees the call, and he opposes you. By the very definition of who he is, he acts and stands in full, combative resistance against you. He knows the mandate, God's plans for you, and opposes them.

He's not a little imp with a red tail and pitchfork grinning slyly at naughtiness. He is pure evil. He is a fallen angel, cast from his presence in God's throne room where he witnessed the wonder and beauty of his Creator yet still rebelled against God's plan for him.

If there is any way he can get you to abort the mission and abdicate the place God has given you, he will. Count on it. He opposes everything God does, and if you are working for God, the devil will oppose you. He will try everything in his power to stop you!

The sooner we learn this, the better armed we are for the level of warfare that arises when we step out of the boat to do anything for God.

chapter nine

Face the Storm

Weathering the disappointments of life without blaming God is of tremendous importance to our faith. To say, "I have just about lost my faith," is to say, "I have just about lost my confidence in Jesus."

In times like that, when our faith in our ideas, inspirations, declarations, and visions vanish, many complaints against the Lord arise from the very lips that once prophesied great things.

"And there arose a great storm of wind, and the waves beat into the ship, so that it was now full" (Mark 4:37). Did you notice the phrase, "the waves beat *into* the ship, so that it was now full" (emphasis added)? This is a desperate situation, a season in which the very lives of these men were in peril—or so it would seem in the natural realm.

Many today have felt the overwhelming flood of adversity, that which would literally fill your ship with doubt, fear, and unbelief. As we look further into the situation of the men in the boat, we see their outcome. "And he was in the hinder part of the ship, asleep on a pillow: and they awake him, and say unto him, 'Master, carest thou not that we perish?'" (Mark 4:38).

This is also often our first response: questioning the Lord's faithfulness when life is unleashed in fury. We wonder where Jesus is. Now the men knew full well that Jesus was aboard their ship; they had boarded with Him. But when the storm came, they—in running to "pray to Jesus"—actually accused Him of not caring. But thankfully, Jesus was not lessened in His resolve or power to deal with the situation.

I am taken with the picture here that describes how we often feel when things get rough. We, too, find Jesus somewhere behind us, a Master who doesn't seem to be leading the way or charting our course very well. And more than that, He's asleep—nice and cushy on a pillow right in the midst of our storm!

"And He arose, and rebuked the wind, and said unto the sea, 'Peace, be still.' And the wind ceased, and there was a great calm" (Mark 4:39). I wondered, as I studied this Scripture, how many times Jesus has also had to rebuke me for my fear and unbelief. Jesus, in questioning the men, is actually teaching them after speaking into the storm and bringing them peace.

"And He said unto them, 'Why are ye so fearful? How is it that ye have no faith?'" (Mark 4:40). Jesus does not beat us up when we are wavering, but takes every opportunity to correct us so we may understand some things when the next time comes.

The journey of faith has some rough spots in the road where we will surely find out what we are made of. These men learned something very important that day. We don't have to learn from our experiences today, we can learn from Jesus' Word to them, which is also a Word to us! We need to check the quality of our faith when troubles come. Do we quickly move into fear, doubt, and unbelief…or do we trust Jesus?

Many times, one of the first things people do when a storm comes is to mutiny, take back the ship, and throw Jesus overboard. Somehow, because we don't know His Word of caution about hardship, we have a high expectation of smooth sailing. When our expectations of Him are dashed in what appears to be His failure to come through for us, we lose our faith in Him. The outflow of relationship with the Captain of our salvation and the Anchor of our faith is having the Master at the helm of our lives. It doesn't matter what the storm is or how difficult the weather patterns we face; we can have confidence in Jesus.

We must keep our faith in Christ's leadership over every endeavor we take on—in the storm and yes, even on calm seas. In fact, it's not just the storm that can bring a challenge to the steadfastness of our faith and trust in Jesus. Smooth sailing can release a great big dose of overconfidence in our own abilities, which is also faithless conduct.

Jesus wants us to put our trust in Him alone—no matter what—even when everything is going right.

chapter ten

This Is Not Utopia!

I have to caution you: The breakthrough we've all been praying for and declaring is going to bring new levels of difficulties with it, even with God moving powerfully. Not everyone is impressed with the move of God in our lives and what we believe Him for, and some will resist it—even withstanding those who cross over to fulfill the promises of God.

I bet you didn't want to hear that, did you? But it is true that difficulties have already risen to confront those who are following the ways of the Lord. Think back to the beginning of the journey and remember the past price of seeking God. Where we are heading will continue to require a price that followers of Christ must pay. Disciples always stir a city, make enemies, and win converts (see Acts 17:4–6).

While the season ahead of us will be glorious, it will also be a time of testing to see how mature and how decided we actually have become.

Breakthrough brings persecution.

Are you ready for this? You may say, "But I have already been suffering enough." All that has suffered so far is dying flesh. The suffering I am talking about now is that which is counted as the joy of being partakers with Christ (see Philippians 3:10).

Does this mean you will have to die?

Maybe not. But it does mean that you have to die to your will to live so that you won't fight against suffering, should it come. It is a form of "selling all to follow Christ"—even to the extent of laying down our lives. That was the determination of the early church. Its members had to be that determined, because the opportunities to cave in to the pressure to conform abounded all around. We, too, will face different kinds of pressure—some from within the walls of our churches, others from our families and friends, and yet others in our governments. And that's not counting the satanic pressures applied to liquidate us.

Some of you out there already know what I am speaking of, especially those in other nations who have already seen the pressure and deep persecution.

Take a look at each of these names:

Jesus—His life was a series of confrontations with the religious world. Everything He did and said created a stir.

John the Baptist—This outspoken forerunner lost his head because he dared to confront sin issues.

Paul and Silas—They were beaten and spent time in prison because of the power of God at work in their lives to set people free as they declared the Name of Jesus.

Stephen—He was stoned to death because of his life and message, even though he was used greatly to spread the gospel, with signs following him.

The martyrs of the church, then and now—Throughout history, certain people have been imprisoned, beaten, and killed for walking out their faith in their everyday lives. Wherever they went, full of the power of God, they shook cities, the strongholds of the enemy, and whatever religious powers were in control of that area. They made many enemies that were bent on killing them—and they eventually did kill many of them.

Most Christians in the modern world are not prepared to face anything other than comfort and plenty. I don't believe the church is prepared to face the difficult times ahead. Yes, the harvest is coming in, but not without a fight for the faith. It will take those who have already decided about the possible consequences of their faith to stand in difficult times.

Just take a look at the disciples in the time that led up to the cross, and then at their own lives as they moved on into breakthrough following Pentecost. It was no picnic, and it is not going to be a picnic for us. We need to get our heads out of the clouds and prepare for this time that is probably going to stretch us farther than we've been stretched in any of the years behind us. Take a look with me at the One who paid the ultimate price:

Gethsemane—This time of prayer brought Jesus the deepest agony over the dedication to the lost souls of humanity. He knew the ultimate cost was His life. However, He spent this time in prayer alone. The disciples slept through this level of agony. This kind of prayer separates those who will go to the garden to pray from those who want to sleep (see Luke 22:40–46).

The Crucifixion—The flesh has to really die or you run away to save the flesh from the pain of death. The death of our dreams will be a challenging time, a testing of our faith: What do we believe? At the cross, there was only Jesus' mother and one disciple–the one who "lay his head upon the breast of Jesus." Only those who are intimate friends of Jesus will get this close to death (see John 19:26–27; Luke 23:33, 49–50; and Mark 15:39).

The Resurrection—You would think that everyone would be overjoyed about life that comes from any grave, but needless to say, not everyone is excited when dreams rise out of the tombs of seeming defeat.

Many a naysayer and the "I-told-you-so-people" will not want to say "hallelujah!" when your victory comes. Jesus' resurrection was met with unbelief, skepticism, and an attempt by many to discredit Him as a hoax (Matthew 27:62–66, 28:11–15).

There are those who want to shut our doors and seal them because they have heard the rumors that "on the third day we, as Jesus did, shall arise and live in His sight"—the doors through which we will arise and walk out of in resurrection power.

And now to us, the modern-day disciples. What about us? Here we are now: the Christians, the Pentecostals, the independents, mainline denominations, churches abounding on many corners of the cities, positioned right in the middle of it all. Someone has to break the barriers of religion to get the gospel of Jesus Christ to the world. And here we are, asking ourselves a lot of tough questions to challenge us to go deeper than just riding on someone else's religion.

Thank God that a group of people know they must stir the waters and jump in for themselves, not waiting for others. They will not be willing to take second-hand encounters, but desire to go face to face with the power of God, as the 120 did on the day of Pentecost.

It was in the midst of Roman government "controlling" the move of God following Pentecost that the "fanatics" were born out of the fires of adversity. They stood out like a sore thumb, but they were convinced that "the enemy" (and especially religion) should not control the destiny of God's people.

May I ask: What will the church of today look like when it is all said and done and our race has been run? What will you and I look like?

I know this is not a "user-friendly" message, but the church has to prepare for the next season. I can't tell you how deeply I feel that we must be prepared to stand in the fires of adversity. This is not to alarm anyone unduly, but to alert us to the condition of the modern church, which has moved far from the original model Jesus set in order. We, as a people, have moved far from the pattern He set up for His disciples to follow. What He asked of them required a lot of change, and it will be no less demanding of us to make changes in our way of "thinking" and "doing" church.

We have to learn to recognize the trait we have to lean

towards the comfort zones of our lives, or we will never challenge ourselves to step forward in our faith—a faith that will take us places we have never been and stretch us in ways we never thought possible.

Too many "corpses" are on the side of the road, as some have just sat down and died, "letting the fire die." You see, at some time, the things we believe deep inside our hearts will tell whether we believe or not.

Do we know how to build a fire and keep it burning, even in the midst of storms, trials, abandonment, persecution, and sifting? If we can take the time to evaluate ourselves at this stage of our lives, then maybe we can guard ourselves against the tragedy of giving up.

Why do people give up? There are too many tests. The time and distance they would have to travel is too far, too hard. They don't like being "peculiar." The scoffers and mockers are too hard to deal with. The change is too much, too fast. The demand of prayer is overwhelming. The warfare is too much. The talk of "dying to the flesh" is a bit too much. The persecution is frightening. The way is too narrow-minded for an open-minded world.

So, I ask: Do you believe, or are you just following the crowd, doing things because someone else is doing it?

God has given all people a challenge to obey Him by doing things His way, to lay down that which is in their hands (including abilities, plans, opinions, concepts, occupations, destiny, money, and goods) and pick up their cross. This speaks of our own self-sufficiency. God is asking for a total sell-out to His Kingdom. He asks us to trust Him with our very lives.

Elusive Faith

The days are upon us when we have to be willing to lay aside everything for the cause of the Kingdom and its King, our Lord and Savior Jesus Christ. It's all a matter of lordship. We are God's people for this time. We just have to plant that so deeply within our hearts that nothing can steal the seed of God's purpose and design for each of us who is an intricate part of that plan.

The Lord spoke this truth into my heart: There is a tendency, if we are not sure of our future, to keep looking at our past.

If perchance you recognize yourself as one who has sat down on the side of the road, feeling like giving up or walking away, but deciding to get back on the right track and move on, then God will give you the helping hand up from your slump. He loves to watch His children get up and keep going in spite of the difficulties and disappointments.

It is not the falling down that bothers Him, but the giving up.

I encourage you to get up, dust yourself off, and simply make up your mind that you are going to come back to the place where you left your destiny, your prayer life, your devotion to the Lord, and your vision, hope, faith, and trust in the One who called you.

You may need to humble yourself before God, ask His forgiveness, and seek strength from Him in the areas of your weaknesses, fears, and doubt, but He is faithful to strengthen us in our weaknesses and create in us an overcoming spirit—if we will just agree with Him. He loves you so much, and His desire for you is greater than you can imagine.

Don't lose confidence in the One who called you and placed you in your harvest field. Here are some suggestions for those who have remained in spite of the difficulties:

Pray for those who are struggling, that their faith may be strengthened.

Pray for churches facing difficult times in hard places.

Pray for intercessors, that they will not lose hope in times of testing and fatigue.

Pray for churches struggling financially and numerically in this season.

Pray for pastors and their wives to stand strong in their cities for the final thrust of the sword to bring "breakthrough to the harvest."

Pray that God will keep the revival pure and focused.

Pray that those who have moved into error will be brought back to the truth.

Pray that the Word of God will build an unshakeable house for those who are pressing in hard after God.

Pray that the youth and children of this age will be delivered from the pull of the world.

Pray for those who are struggling, that they will be strengthened in their hearts to keep going.

Pray that you, yourself, will endure as a good soldier.

chapter eleven

Showdown

Many showdowns have taken place in biblical history, but none with such rippling effects as what took place when the children of Israel were at the brink of crossing over into the new land.

Showdown: "An event, especially a confrontation that forces an issue to a conclusion."

The results of a showdown have dramatic significance. In fact, whole nations have had their courses changed after showdowns—and so have churches, families, and yes, even cities.

A showdown occurred in Israel's history as the Israelites arrived at the Jordan River. God had set His people free from Egyptian captivity, and had brought them to Himself. They were physically moving, but their "inner man" was still divided. He had dealt with His people several times to free them from the shackles of fleshpots and the golden calf that was still intertwined in their minds and hearts, which had brought division time and again to the camp.

They had journeyed hard and long, following Moses according to the Word of God. They had seen the hand of God move mightily in miraculous ways. They had been protected and spared as God had spoiled the enemy's camp, destroying the enemy army in the Red Sea. They had seen God deal with the rebellion of Korah, they had seen how He had dealt with the golden calf raised up in the wilderness, and they had witnessed the bloody execution of many people as a result of that gross error. They had gone through a plague that placed them on the verge of extinction.

Those who had survived to this point knew God up close and personal on many levels, including His promises to them. These were not people who did not know the bottom line. Every step of the journey they had taken rang with the promises. And now, they were on the cusp of attaining those promises. They had been brought to the very place where God had destined for them to cross over. And this, too, would be a place of testing. I don't believe God was shocked at what happened next, but He was not happy about it (or tolerant of it), either.

He brought them to the dividing line where the hearts of "those who will" and "those who won't" were revealed. Twelve men were sent in to scope out the land, to survey what lay before them. They were like the scouts of old who went ahead of the wagon train in the early days of America's existence. The difference was that they already knew the way it was, long before they got there.

When the Israelite scouts went in, they shouldn't have been surprised at what they saw; they should have been shocked if it wasn't exactly as God had said it would be. Here are the facts: All of the men of Israel sent in to spy out the land knew this was the place God had talked about in His prophetic Word:

> And I am come down to deliver them out of the hand of the Egyptians, and to bring them up out of that land unto a good land and a large, unto a land flowing with milk and honey; unto the place of the Canaanites, and the Hittites, and the Amorites, and the Perizzites, and the Hivites, and the Jebusites.
>
> Exodus 3:8

God told His people how wonderful the land was, and He listed the enemy combatants of the land where He would take them. Here is what they stated after getting an up-close and very personal view of the land: "And they told him, and said, 'We came unto the land whither thou sentest us, and surely it floweth with milk and honey; and this is the fruit of it'" (Numbers 13:27).

They even held in their hands the evidence that this was the place God had chosen for them: the grapes, figs, and pomegranates, the fruit of the land, huge and in abundance. They stated, "This is the land that flows with milk and honey, just as you told us, but…"

> Nevertheless the people be strong that dwell in the land, and the cities are walled, and very great: and moreover we saw the children of Anak there. The Amalekites dwell in the land of the south: and the Hittites, and the Jebusites, and the Amorites, dwell in the mountains: and the Canaanites dwell by the sea, and by the coast of Jordan.
>
> Numbers 13:28–29

I can just see a little kid gasping for air as he elaborates on the story of how the dog chased him home. As he tells the story, the dog gets bigger and bigger until it's the size of a bear. No doubt with their eyes wide, God's people say, "They're strong—*gasp!*—and the cities are walled—*gasp!*—and huge—*gasp!*—and the giants live in that land—*gasp!*—and all the other bad guys are on every side from one side to the other—*gasp, gasp,* and *gasp!*"

Well, yes, these spies were telling the truth. Actually, they were now quoting the prophecy by sight; it was exactly as God had said it would be. However, with the same breath, they declared the hopelessness of the situation. It was no longer just a prophetic word about the inhabitants of the land; they were very real, very many, very big, and very strong!

You see, sometimes we mentally and emotionally paint the end of the journey like a rainbow-dream ending. We anxiously wait for the golden harvest to come in and for the joys that await us when that happens, but do we really know that when we invade enemy territory for those souls, we will face some "bad guys" in the process of taking possession?

You think the children of Israel came out with problems; wait until you see what comes with the last-days harvest. It is going to be a battle for souls!

You will be cleaning fish that are slippery, slimy, and hard to hang onto—without the grace of God. These people are not going to just slide into your nice, comfortable pews and sit with calm smiles on their faces as they join your church. NO! You are going to have to invade enemy territory, the new land filled with giants. But God's promise says, "You win because He is going to go before you!"

It's back to God's propensity to give you a mountainous problem to face, and your knowing that He's in it with you because

He said so. If we do not believe this, we will wilt in the face of the disappointment that "the bad guys" really do exist in our Promised Land. Oh yes, we still quote the wonderful saying, "the land of milk and honey," as if we have never read the rest of the story.

Is this going to be some of us? Will the Lord reveal the size of our battle in the new land, and then when we see it, we too will draw back as if we were not expecting it to be "like this"? Can't you just feel the fear rippling through the congregation as the picture was painted so grimly by "Big-Mouth Doubt," by the overwhelming flood of the majority voice?

Thank God for the voice that still resounds with the promise that rises up in the midst of the loud mouths, raising a banner of victory against the foes of defeat, despair, and disappointment.

Caleb's voice was infused with the vision and promises of God rising up to still those who simply didn't get that God was going to use them for His glory in a big land with big problems. "And Caleb stilled the people before Moses, and said, 'Let us go up at once, and possess it; for we are well able to overcome it'" (Numbers 13:30). Caleb is the counter-offensive voice in this showdown of "do we or don't we?"

Look at the definition of the word, *yakol* (*Strong's* 3201), which is the Hebrew word for both "we are well able" and "overcome": "To prevail, to overcome, to endure, to have power, to be able to gain or accomplish, to be able to endure, to be able to reach, to prevail over or against, to overcome, to be victor, to have ability, to have strength."

Caleb is dealing a double-punch blow to doubt, fear, and unbelief. He said, *"Yakol, yakol!"*—"We are well able; we can prevail.

We have the strength; we are able to accomplish the task at hand, to overcome, to prevail, to have strength, to be able to accomplish the task at hand."

Why is same word used two times? It is an emphatic pronouncement over the negativity being spread among the people: "But the men that went up with him said, 'We be not able to *[yakol]* go up against the people; for they are stronger than we.'"

The Dissenting Voice

All you have to do is add a "no" to the right word structure and it turns into a negative very fast. Caleb said, "We are well able," and the others said, "We are not able." Then they qualified the problem they were having with where God had led them. To top it off, they painted an even bleaker picture, one so bad in God's ears that He called it an "evil report":

> And they brought up an evil report of the land which they had searched unto the children of Israel, saying, "The land, through which we have gone to search it, is a land that eateth up the inhabitants thereof; and all the people that we saw in it are men of a great stature."
>
> NUMBERS 13:32

Just a minute. "Eats up the inhabitants of the land"? That is not a part of the prophecy! How often do we exaggerate the situation, just like this? This is a slippery slope with God. We need to say things the way He says them.

As they continued, they stated, "And there we saw the giants, the sons of Anak, which come of the giants: and we were in our own sight as grasshoppers, and so we were in their sight" (Numbers 13:33).

I want us to really take a close look at the comparison here of the Israelite scouts and the inhabitants of the land with giants and grasshoppers. I don't know why we would take the vessel God has called out to use—meaning us—and belittle ourselves by saying we're impotent to do what He has asked. When we do that, comparing ourselves to the giants as if we were grasshoppers, we also diminish God's power—not in heaven, but on earth. Oh, He's still strong, but His instruments on earth are cursing themselves as weaklings, totally inept, powerless, and fearful.

Do we even know the power of God that has been invested in us to work through us in the place of our calling and bring everything He's invested in us to a conclusion, to His glory and honor? The Bible tells us of the giants of the land, giving us measurements by which we may evaluate their size alongside the average human being.

"There were giants in the earth in those days" (Genesis 6:4). Deuteronomy 3:11 states that the bed of Og, king of Bashan, was nine cubits by four cubits (approximately fourteen feet long by six feet wide). These giants were called "Nephilim," which in English means "a giant bully or tyrant." Yes, these were big, mean killing machines!

To see giants up close and personal must have been overwhelming to unbelieving minds. These men were reporting that they saw people of superhuman strength and size. This so overwhelmed them that they stated, "All the people are giants!"

It must have been an impressive sight to stand there as men of normal height and look at a mountain of men. But if they had looked higher, they would have seen what loomed above the heads of the giants. God's Word was poised over that land, over the heads of the giants, over the strongholds of the enemy.

Nothing can be higher or more potent than the Word of the Living God! Our reports must say what God has said, not what we see. We are well able. It's not because we are so great but because God is so great.

We can either carry the Word of the Lord around in our minds with casual acceptance in an easy time, or we can plant it deep into our spirits to prepare us for difficult times ahead, just as God said they would be.

Where that Word is being carried is essential to survival at the moment of challenge. We can generate all kinds of valid-sounding reasons for our arguments: too big, too far out, too overwhelming, too scary…

Why didn't Caleb and Joshua come out fear-filled and not just doubting, but refusing like the others to partake of the battle for the Promised Land? They looked at the same thing the other spies did, but they walked out filled with faith, gripping the Word of God, hanging on to the promise He had given them to overthrow every king, village, and mountaintop dweller of the new land. They were ready to go in obedience to possess the land.

I say again, as Caleb did to a people so long ago, "You are well able!"

You will face the giants of the land. You will face your Jericho. Your little feeble body, compared to those giants, will look outsized and overpowered—and maybe in the natural realm, that is exactly the way it is. But in the Spirit of God, that is not the way it is.

You are caught up in a plan that is way over your head, but you are part of the incredible hand of God moving. Your eyes will see what God sees and know what He knows. He will ask you to sing a song to drop the wall. He will ask you to use a stone in a sling to drop a giant. Your part may appear puny in the eyes of man, but in God's sight, the song He asks you to sing is a bunker-busting bomb and the stone is a high-powered, heat-seeking missile, programmed by the hand of God to hit the target.

Yes, a giant is taller than you, outweighs you, and has a very convincing voice with which to mock you, but your God, the One who is greater in you than the one in the world, has omnipotence and a voice of thunder and lightning.

He, in you, ripples your flesh with His power!

The truth is, when God gives you a word and direction, you are well able to do it. He doesn't choose losers. He chooses ordinary people of ordinary stature to be called out to all kinds of fields of engagement to win.

Part IV

Push, Press, and Pray!

"You've not yet prayed like you're going to pray!"
—Loren Dummer

chapter twelve

Beachhead

Take some time with me, right here in the middle of our journey through this book, to emphasize the importance of prayer and warfare.

A beachhead is a small plot of land that serves as a staging area for attacking the enemy. It is so strategic that the enemy will do anything to prevent one from being established.

It is established at a very high cost. It is held at a cost. It must not be relinquished at any price or for any cause!

We've seen the loss and casualties of the past years, but many of God's people did not lie down and die in the wilderness. They will cross over and take hold of the promise God has given them.

It is time to move into the latter-day beachhead.

When Joshua crossed over with the children of Israel, they went up against Jericho, a fortressed city built as an impenetrable wall against any encroachment. But God was on the move with a people who knew the strength of obedience and faithfulness to the call to possess the land. God brought down the walls without casualties of war.

You might be facing your Jericho and wondering how in the world you are going to break through. You will do it the same way God has been doing things all along: You will go against the walls in the name of the LORD of Hosts, in the power and might of the Spirit of God.

You will worship and pray your way to breakthrough. There's no other way.

We all want to think there is something we must do to "huff and puff, and blow the house of the enemy down," but God is the breath needed, and He can be found breathing in our intercession, high praise, worship, and prophecy.

The children of Israel were specifically instructed not to go out in their own roar, but to keep silent until God said to shout. Only at that time could the roar of the Lion of Judah be heard. The people inside the walls already feared the God of Israel; they had heard of His power and defense of those who now surrounded them.

They didn't say, "We saw Joshua coming and were really frightened." They didn't say they were scared of Israel. They said they were frightened of the God of Israel.

Those who survive the wilderness are ready to land on the front steps of the enemy encampment sitting in the middle of the promise. There are people who will do what God has called them to do, whatever that may be.

It is a time for the fearless, not the fearful, a time for the faithful, not the faithless, to go forth in high praise and prayer, with direct hits against the walls that oppose them! We need to have a mantle called "fervent and effectual prayer" (James 5:16) resting on us. God needs winners, people who know how to carry on the journey to the point of breakthrough.

Prophetic accuracy must fall on the church and then prophetic obedience must follow as we pray, declare, and indeed move the prophetic through to fulfillment. Get a picture of the church of the future. Know what it is to look like, for you are it!

chapter thirteen

Faithful, Frustrated, and Fallen

> "Wherefore seeing we also are compassed about with so great a cloud of witnesses, let us lay aside every weight, and the sin which doth so easily beset us, and let us run with patience the race that is set before us."
>
> Hebrews 12:1

This speaks of a remarkable group of people who stepped onto the pages of heavenly history. Some of their names are recorded, while others are nameless. If it were not for these people and the multitude who have followed them through the ages, the earth would be very different than it is today.

What difference does a single intercessor make on the earth, and what would happen if all intercession was removed? This is a very disturbing thought. Imagine a sudden and full removal of all intercession from the entire earth. Imagine the results if prayer were removed from the lips of every human being.

What would the world look like? What would happen to families? What would happen in governments and the nations of the world? What would happen to our sons' and daughters' futures? What would happen to the churches and the people of God?

Imagine families no longer held together by prayer and schools being turned over to a reprobate system as the mind of the enemy, unrestrained, invades the minds of our students.

Imagine terrorists moving unhindered into nations of the world, massive death and losses hitting in devastating blow after blow, with no room to breathe.

Imagine the grossest of sins speeding in their advance on our youth and children as all of hell's best drugs, schemes, and rebellion are released in full impact.

Imagine the spirit of abortion moving unrestrained against the children in the womb and incest and abuse of all kinds ravaging the children of the earth beyond measure.

Imagine the wars that would break out in every nation, and the resulting loss of life because no one is protected in battle.

Imagine the crime that would rampage on the streets as fear grips the hearts of people locked behind closed doors.

Imagine gangs wreaking havoc on cities and little towns as the mutated souls of these warriors are perverted to the lowest level of rebellion and hatred.

Imagine the demonic forces of the enemy moving without any censorship, spewing their demonic and vile vomit on the earth.

Imagine the books, movies, Internet, music, and entertainment industries without any competition for the hearts and souls of people.

Imagine every fire going out and every river running dry, with no waterfalls, rain, fish, harvest, prophetic Word, worship, or altars—churches dying and closing their doors, with no movement of the Spirit of God.

Imagine no more tears of repentance or sorrow for sin, only tears of bitterness and unforgiveness as the souls of man withdraw from the cross.

Now imagine all of this all being unleashed at the same time like a black, hate-filled cloud of destruction bent on destroying the last breath of God in man by killing until no one is left—a rampage of evil such as the world has never known, not even in the Dark Ages. It is a sudden and full implosion of planet earth's inhabitants as they cave in on themselves when the unleashed evil and terror are no longer held back by intercession.

Am I painting a bleak picture that is passionately overplayed by my imagination and emotions? I do not believe so, for there will be a time when the church will no longer be on earth praying. The prayer movements will be gone. The river of God will draw its banks back to the throne from which it cascaded to earth. The Spirit of God will not be covering the face of the earth with the glory of God the way it does today. Churches will probably be filled, but with those who are running for safety that is no longer present on earth or in the church, seeking refuge at altars void of the ones who cried tears there.

I imagine there will be a strange sense of loneliness on earth when many realize their praying mamas, daddies, pastors, friends, or siblings are gone. A kind of silence will be released. Sometimes, silence is deafening. These people will hear shrieks of silence echoing around the world. And yes, the earth will experience God's wrath, for no godly intercessors will be left to stand in the gap and make up the hedge.

What I am describing is only a drop in the bucket of the evil that will come out of the Antichrist's rule and reign of terror and torment.

But it is not that time yet!

We do have people praying—just not enough.

We do have those who have continued to press in, but some have fallen away.

We do have spiritual earthquakes in response to prayer, but many places are still silent with no one on the wall of mercy and grace. There are churches without intercessions, and the world already shows in them. There are families without intercessors, and the damage to the family line is so deep that recovery of the heritage God meant for them can only come through prayer.

If prayer goes, every vital, life-giving force ceases as well because it is the only line of communication between God and man. Intercession is Holy-Spirit praying through God's church for the cry of God's heart: souls! It is sounded as war at times and as weeping at others, but the sounds of intercession, offered by those who stand in the gap, must rise to God's ears instead of the vulgarity of mankind, who is cursing God daily. God must hear us instead of the insulting idolatry that releases sound from the four corners of the earth, sounds of perversion and corruption of all kinds.

Intercession holds back destruction and demons, and ebbs humanity's natural pull towards the lowest level of living. We are not stopping it all, but a greater impact is being made than we can even begin to realize. The sounds of intercession grip the heart of God.

I felt the Holy Spirit taking this challenge deeper yet…

Now, imagine the results if just *your* prayers of intercession were to cease!

God pointed out to me that it is a "person-by-person call," and if any of us is not filling our prayer closets with intercession, then something is uncovered: something fails, or something dies. While there is a powerful move around the world today, many are missing in action.

I believe God is making a call across the nations to return to prayer. The battle has been long and hard, and many have suffered some terrible blows for many reasons, but God is still faithful to restore. I believe there are those who have had the "want to" taken out of them by circumstances and the enemy, but God can replace their hearts for the battle and restore what the enemy has taken.

You are actually a more seasoned warrior now that you have learned the pitfalls of intercession, and you are more valuable than ever to the Lord. You have learned powerful lessons that are needed on the field of intercession.

Mistakes should teach us but should not kill us.

Here are two questions to ponder from opposite sides of the spectrum:

- What if everyone was faithful?
- What if everyone quit?

I would like to hold out for the first option and believe that God will revive His powerful move in your spirit that once burned there. Whether you have become a casualty, you are just tired and discouraged, or if you are currently standing strong, I encourage you to move "forwards ever; backwards never!" Thrive on the wall!

I would like to share this dream with you. May the Lord encourage your heart in that He knows where you are.

In my dream, the Lord was showing me a memorial wall, similar to the Vietnam Veterans Memorial Wall in Washington DC, though smaller and belonging to a people in whom God had greatly moved in intercession. Names were inscribed of those who died in battle: people whom God raised up to intercede for revival, the harvest, deliverance, their cities, their churches, and such.

I saw names I recognized on the wall. These were names of people who had been removed from active duty—some by "enemy fire" and others by "friendly fire." The shrapnel of criticism, the land mines of accusation, bullets of jealousy, and missiles of division—an arsenal of weapons, carnal and demonic in nature, had been unleashed against them.

I saw a certain man arrogantly leaning in disrespect upon the wall, showing no honor for the sacrifice of those inscribed thereon. I recognized him as one who had been used by the enemy to do great harm to the cause of Christ, bringing personal injury to those being used by God in prayer and warfare. Every time God had begun to move, this man had made a counter-move.

I realized the grief of God in the matter that these were people in His army listed here. He who enlists the one who will stand in the gap and make up the hedge was saddened and angry to see them assaulted by religious spirits in the church.

The results of this action were that those being used by God in intercession came under such criticism that they began to suffer greatly. No, they didn't die physically, but the death of intercession on any level is a great loss to the Kingdom of God.

The message I got from this is that we need to reach back

and pick up some fallen warriors who are no longer standing in the gap and making up the hedge. I felt in my dream that we needed a resurrection at this wall and at walls around the world. We should not eulogize these names for what they once were! Though I felt sorrow, I also felt I should not cry at the wall or grieve at their passing, but call out to the names on the wall to rise up to live again!

The stories I am hearing of intercessors leaving prayer behind and even walking away from friends, pastors, and churches is alarming. The battlefield is littered with the wounded, and the wall is filled with names.

If you have been wounded, please forgive and let Jesus heal your wounds. Pull out the arrows of offense and unforgiveness and let all bitterness go so you can rise up to live and serve God again.

Oh, you say, "I am still serving God, just not that way." Once called to this level of entrustment, you can never escape the call. The voice of the Lion of the Tribe of Judah will be a haunting sound in your ears until you "run to the roar!"

chapter fourteen

Holy Desperation

Though we live in a fallen world, we are not fallen people. I am talking to people who have set their sights on a higher plain than the natural realm.

I must not enter any encounter with God with any mindset less than that of an overcomer and victor. We have to find the path the Holy Spirit is on and go there. The only way to go there is to follow the Holy Spirit.

We must get used to tuning our ears to the voice of the Spirit so we will hear His voice in the midst of the many other voices that vie for our attention. We have to shut out everything, deliberately and completely, in order to tune in to the frequency in which Holy Spirit is speaking.

We cannot be passive.

We cannot be distracted.

We cannot be fireless.

We have to actively seek God with a passion and fire that will drive us forward in response to His Spirit. The Holy Spirit wants to direct our attention to the Lord Jesus Christ, who is at the right hand of the Father, making intercession for us.

When we come before Him, whether He is dressed for war, wearing a crown and holding a sword, or dressed to sit down and dine with us, we have to be ready to meet Him on His terms.

As good soldiers, we must always be ready.

As worshippers, we must always be ready.

As prophetic people, we must always be ready.

The Lord is waiting on us!

I hear a sound every time I prepare to lead prayer, but so far I have only heard it in my spirit. It is not a noise, it is a sound. It comes from prayer warriors. It is filled with hunger, longing, desire, reaching, and desperation—and cries that have yet to be released.

Yes, we pray, and we have prayed and moved heaven's heart as we got the heartbeat of God in focus, but this sound is yet to be released in this revival. It no doubt was released in revivals past.

Maybe we are not desperate enough or hungry enough yet.

I sometimes listen at prayer time to see if we have accessed a level of prayer that will break us open with travailing intercession. Not noise, but a sound of the Spirit of God crying out and groaning from deep within our spirits. These prayers cannot be muttered mindlessly because we know the words, nor can they come from our minds, because we cannot author them. It is not a sound of numbers or quantity, as when we sometimes think that the large crowds who make a mighty noise are reaching out farther than those of us who are small in number. It is about the quality of prayer—the kind that extends beyond us into a realm of spirit praying that will give the final thrust of the sickle into the harvest and break the awakening that we have long desired and prayed for.

I recall the words that came from the Lord, "You have not yet prayed like you're going to pray…"

I know it is coming.

God is preparing His church to pray so as to break open a well of untapped prayer, prayer that to this point has not yet been heard in this revival. We need to always be ready for that infusion of Spirit-led praying as the disciples were prepared in the upper room on the day of Pentecost.

chapter fifteen

Appearances Can Be Deceiving

Many people in many places have embraced intercession as an active part of their relationship with God. Intercession comes as a natural part of the move of God, the promise of God.

We have received a call to step out to the place of God's leading, whether we are physically in one place or are moving from place to place around the country or nations.

Thankfully, movement is not about what our bodies do; it's about being in position wherever God has called us to be and His moving there. It is because we dare to step our feet onto this ground of promise that the enemy has declared to be his own, that we face a battle of significant proportions. We do face a wall of resistance in going after the harvest for the Kingdom of God. That is why we refer to those who intercede as prayer warriors.

The enemy would like for all of us to wave the flag of surrender. Oh, how easy that would be at times! Yet how could we walk out on God? He has prepared us, invested in us, and positioned us in specific places and with unique assignments. The season we are in is taxing, but we cannot intercede with the mindset we had before we understood the things we now know. God has birthed in His people who have believed Him new insight and trained ears to hear what the Spirit is saying to the churches. He has trained our hands to war and has taught our fingers to fight. He has prepared us to cross over and take every square inch of land He wants.

The fatigue and discouragement at times are very real and encompassing, but God is faithful. Lifting the arms of other warriors weary from the battle is a responsibility and a privilege for us.

Sometimes it appears that all is lost; the dream is dead, the vision has dimmed, and the grave has snatched our hopes from us. Look at what one might describe as the darkest day on earth. Or was it?

> And, behold, there was a man named Joseph, a counselor; and he was a good man, and a just: (The same had not consented to the counsel and deed of them;) he was of Arimathaea, a city of the Jews: who also himself waited for the kingdom of God. This man went unto Pilate, and begged the body of Jesus. And he took it down, and wrapped it in linen, and laid it in a sepulchre that was hewn in stone, wherein never man before was laid. And that day was the preparation, and the Sabbath drew on. And the women also, which came with him from Galilee, followed after, and beheld the sepulcher, and how His body was laid.
>
> LUKE 23:50–55

To all appearances, death permeated the space Joseph and the women moved in as they wrapped up their dream of a powerful move of God and prepared to bury it.

They had seen the greatest move of God ever! They had experienced the most profound teachings and miracles! They had been walking and talking with Jesus in communion and friendship; hope was high with a bright outlook for their future. They believed in this Jesus as the Messiah who had changed their whole world. Their old religion was dead and behind them as they moved into the New Covenant, something they had heard prophesied for so long.

These disciples had vision, excitement, and high expectations for their future. They had begun to understand the messages and parables, and had asked questions and received answers that made sense.

They were growing in their faith in Jesus.

When Joseph asked for the body of Jesus, he picked up the lifeless form of all their dreams and plans, the lifeless form of the Messiah they had all embraced as the Son of God. You see, this was one part of Jesus' message they never understood. They had not understood the part about His dying, much less the part about His rising up again on the third day.

We all experience trials of our faith when we wonder where Jesus is, but we've never really seen Him buried. In the backs of our minds, we know that He rose from the dead; we're just not sure He's risen from the dead for our area of concern.

People today have a hard time in the church when the smallest trials come, but if there's ever a time when our world and faith are shaken, that's when our dreams die. Think of all the planning and preparation that had taken place as the disciples walked and talked with Jesus. And now, for what?

Joseph laid Jesus in the tomb. The women who came with him from Galilee followed, and "beheld the sepulcher and how the body of Jesus was laid."

Then they went to church.

Can you imagine what that service must have been like? We've all suffered some losses, but nothing like the day Jesus was crucified. How do you praise God when Jesus, the Messiah, the hope of the world, is dead?

This was a severe trial.

No matter how much Jesus had prepared them, they still were not ready to have it end. Their lives had been so entwined with Jesus that we can only imagine the vacancy.

I guess this is why I wonder…

How can people experience a powerful move of God and then not grieve when it's dead?

How can they go back to nominal worship?

How can they adjust back to living in the shallows of having nothing left?

How can they settle back down after the miracles, the salvations, the things they had witnessed and experienced?

The church should be grieving the death of the move of God, the death of the vision, the grave where hopes and dreams are buried under a wrap of religion. I believe there are people who feel as if they just buried something so dear to them, and there is a grief that the move of God in their midst appears to be over. Everyone around seems content to bury the dead and go on with life, but you just can't let it go like this. There has to be more…

> Now upon the first day of the week, very early in the morning, they came unto the sepulcher, bringing the spices which they had prepared, and certain others with them. And they found the stone rolled away from the

sepulcher. And they entered in, and found not the body of the Lord Jesus.

And it came to pass, as they were much perplexed thereabout, behold, two men stood by them in shining garments: And as they were afraid, and bowed down their faces to the earth, they said unto them, "Why seek ye the living among the dead? He is not here, but is risen: remember how He spoke unto you when He was yet in Galilee, Saying, 'The Son of man must be delivered into the hands of sinful men, and be crucified, and the third day rise again.'"

And they remembered His words, And returned from the sepulcher, and told all these things unto the eleven, and to all the rest.

Luke 24:1–9

There are people who stay close to a dying/dead move of God, just in case something happens. It is not settled in their minds that this is all there is to it.

They remember the call to follow Jesus.

They remember the glory days and will not let go of them.

They remember the days of bread and wine and still have a taste for them.

They remember the sound of Jesus' voice and long to hear Him speak.

All the past memories are not going to do for these people. They will not settle in their hearts that it is over. They will not let the thing lay buried, but they strive in faith to hang onto the vision they received from this Man Jesus.

Pastors, intercessors, and ministry people all through God's church have had a vision, walked and talked with Jesus, smelled the fragrance, and felt the power and presence of this Man—and they will not let any of it go!

These are desperate days for desperate people who are willing to go to the grave and stay there, looking inside until the earthquake opens that grave and releases the vision once again that this is truly Christ, the Son of the Living God. It is not a time to slack off, give up, and go home. There's no better time than now to visit the grave and see the resurrection of all we thought was dead.

Resurrection is not about us unwrapping anything. It's about the power of God breaking open the grave and revealing the life He is still breathing into the move of God, the call of God, the vision, prophecy, and promises of God!

God gave our church a word in mid-2009, telling us, "You are not the only ones I have. I have many others just like you all over the world faithful, prepared, and ready for me to use in this season that is fast approaching."

There are churches still faithful to their calling and moving powerfully forward.

There are pastors who have paid the deep price for their desire for God to move in the church.

There are prophets speaking, decreeing, and declaring the Word of God in purity and truth.

There are worship leaders prophesying in song, leading the church forward in the spirit-and-truth worship that enthrones Jesus.

There are evangelists knocking on the doors of the church and asking to enter to help pull in the harvest in towns and cities, preaching with a passion for the souls Jesus died to save.

There are intercessors standing in places all over the nation, filling prayer closets with weeping and travail for a national revival.

There are missionaries on foreign soil still plowing the ground and planting seed, and waiting.

These are moving forward on their knees, compelled by hunger, praying for revival in the church and the nations, and praying for the great harvest of souls. These all move with great authority and power for tearing down strongholds and building God's Kingdom. They are literally shaking hell's gates to see souls freed.

For those I lift my voice and pray that you will not give up or grow weary as you press into the face of strongholds, push into the presence of God, and persevere in prayer.

The battle cry for the long haul is…"Push, press, and pray!"

chapter sixteen

The Knot People

Prophecy Given by Pastor Loren Dummer
March 23, 2001

> The Spirit of the Lord says,
> "Get ready church. Get ready church.
> Children of Zion, get ready."

You're about to grab in your other hand another instrument. You think that all that you've been doing is fighting a battle against devils and demons. You think that all you've been doing is pushing, pushing, and pushing against strongholds. Though you have been doing this, there has been more. You have been building a net. In the heavenlies, you have been building a net.

In every city across the land, I have a people. I have a remnant.

And in each place they represent **a knot.**

A people that will not quit.
They'll not give up.
They'll not turn back.
They'll not give in.
They'll not go away.
They're a knot people.

And there is a weaving taking place across the land. This net is bigger than what you could have ever imagined.

It doesn't just cover cities.
It doesn't just cover regions.
It covers states.
My net is big.

You're waiting for a purpose. You keep saying, "When? How long? How long? How long?" I've heard it, not just from you, but from across the land I've heard it. People are crying out, "How long, O Lord? How long?"
Get ready, church.
Though you will not lay down your sword as a warrior, you're about to pick up your cleaning tools because fish are about to be caught in the net! **When the time is right** and I say **"now"** to the hosts of heaven, who even now I have strategically placed around the land, they are soon to let go of the net, and the net will fall and it will catch a harvest!

But when the net hits the ground, it will cause a

ripple that will sweep from the Northwest across the land. A ripple will begin to spread. You'll be so busy that you won't have time to look and to ask, "What's going on over here, or what's going on over there? What's happening in this town and what's happening in that town and this church and that church?"

For you shall be so busy in your own harvest.

There are fish that are about to be caught. There is a net (and some of you can now even see it, for I've opened the eyes of some), and even now you see this net stretched across the Northwest and it is about to drop.

It is about to drop.

I said it's about to drop!

Get rid of the unnecessary.

Lay aside the weight, the sin that does so easily beset you.

Turn away from the distractions and get again your focus, for it's about to happen, church.

Children of Zion, it's about to happen.

I've not been just preparing you here, but I've been preparing a people everywhere.

And so I say again what I said at the beginning, "Get ready."

Think about the words "get ready" and ask yourself, "What must I do to be ready?"

You're about to see the most awesome manifestation of God's glory and God's power break forth, "For as lightning strikes from the heavens, so shall my power strike this land," saith the Lord!

Though this word was given over the Pacific Northwest, we believe God has given very similar prophecies all over the nations, gathering to Himself a people of faith and vision, a "knot people" who are willing to be tied in with God's plans by God's hands.

God identified specific "knots" He had tied to form a harvest net. This net was being developed to prevent the loss of what was closest to God's heart: the fish—the souls of men, women, boys, girls, and youth.

Consider your placement in this net as being one strand of many cords knotted into the whole plan of God as you meditate on the following Scripture:

> Two are better than one; because they have a good reward for their labour. For if they fall, the one will lift up his fellow: but woe to him that is alone when he falleth; for he hath not another to help him up. Again, if two lie together, then they have heat: but how can one be warm alone? And if one prevail against him, two shall withstand him; and a threefold cord is not quickly broken.
>
> ECCLESIASTES 4:9–12

God has given us a mandate along with our promise. A promise is not some stagnant, impotent, airy thing floating around out in space; it is God's Word. So a mandate comes to mobilize us.

Look at the definition of mandate:

Mandate (*Strong's* 1501), from Latin *mandatum:* "Commission, order," *mandare:* "to order, commit to one's charge." Literally, "to give into one's hand," probably from *manus:* "hand" (an authoritative order or command); any contract by which a person undertakes to perform services for another.

God decrees a particular thing, such as revival in the church or an awakening in a region or a mission field somewhere. He then releases commissions to individuals, to ministries, to churches, and to intercessors, mandating them to act on His behalf in regards to churches, towns, cities, states, nations, regions, and people. When they answer the call to be an ambassador for heaven, they then act on behalf of God. It is not just about a person or a ministry, but it is about the people of God, worldwide, who move in concert with each other for the glory of the One who called them to serve Him. This is what the harvest net is made of—mandated, faithful people.

This is about a God and a people who play for keeps—to do something that is a permanent and serious move. This is about the strength of the cord, the knots that are tied.

And then there comes a personal commitment that harmonizes with both the promise and the mandate. So the three-strand cord of our heart, mind, and spirit are the promise (God's Word to us), the mandate (our commission), and our commitment (our promise to God).

Consider the following commitment:

We agree to walk together and to work together.

We agree to finish to course.

We agree on revival, just as Jesus has spoken it.

We agree we will hold our position in the spiritual until the release in the natural.

We agree to be bound together for strength.

We agree that we are responsible for the mandate.

We agree we will play for keeps.

We agree we will reach prophetic destination!

Part V

A Fresh Revelation of Christ

"And I turned to see the voice that spake with me. And being turned, I saw seven golden candlesticks; And in the midst of the seven candlesticks one like unto the Son of man, clothed with a garment down to the foot, and girt about the paps with a golden girdle. His head and His hairs were white like wool, as white as snow; and His eyes were as a flame of fire; And His feet like unto fine brass, as if they burned in a furnace; and His voice as the sound of many waters. And He had in His right hand seven stars: and out of His mouth went a sharp two-edged sword: and His countenance was as the sun shineth in His strength."

Revelation 1:12–16

chapter seventeen

The Omega Christ

> " 'I am Alpha and Omega, the beginning and the ending,
> saith the Lord, which is, and which was,
> and which is to come, the Almighty.' "
>
> REVELATION 1:8

Jesus is eternal whether or not you ever met Him, whether or not your path ever crossed His. He was, and is, and is to come. He existed, still exists, and will yet exist long after man has played all his games, done all his deeds, and been judged for the same. *He is.*

The *only* thing we, individually, have to decide is what we will do with Jesus as our lives intersect with His.

Decisions are always made at that place of meeting.

Many people have met Jesus and gave mental consent to the fact of the meeting, but went on down the road a different way. Many have met Jesus in salvation and got stuck right there, never maturing in their faith, never getting to know Jesus. Many have met Jesus and decided to follow Him—all the way—either to the grave or to the return of Christ.

One thing is for sure: The Jesus you met at salvation did not remain in your fixed position with Him. He's moved on—all the way—with a people who are following Him, whatever the cost, come what may.

Whether we burst open a grave at the sound of the trumpet or we are caught up to meet Him in the air, changed in the twinkling of an eye, we will meet the Jesus of the Last Days—not the Babe in the manger, the Jesus on the cross, or even the Jesus out of the tomb. We will be meeting the Jesus who just stepped from the right hand of the Father through the portals of heaven back into our world, up close and personal, and in living color.

John, the one to whom Jesus Christ came while he was on the Isle of Patmos, had an encounter with Jesus so powerful it altered the rest of his life. His visitation was not by a man, but by Jesus Christ—not in flesh, but in glory! It was a fresh revelation of Christ, one that would bring this man to His knees like never before.

John's view of Jesus was one of a human being for most of his earthly relationship with Him. He had walked and talked with Jesus. He had laid his head upon His chest. He had touched His flesh body, one just like his. This was truly an *alpha* relationship, the beginning of knowledge. He had known Him in the veil of His flesh, the Son of Mary, raised in Nazareth.

But this was not who stood before Him on this day…

John had honored Him, stayed close to Him, and been discipled by Him. He had seen Him walk on water, heal the sick, raise the dead, cleanse lepers, heal blind eyes, and restore withered limbs, accomplishing many miracles of great magnitude.

But this still was not the manifestation of the One who came to Him this day. He had gone with Jesus to the Garden of

Gethsemane, seen the arrest, watched Jesus go to the cross and die, seen Him buried and resurrected, and watched Him ascend back into heaven. Nothing could have been more powerful than seeing Jesus walking and talking after being dead and buried. Nothing could have been greater than watching Him go up in clouds of glory. This man had seen things that would blow the minds of average believers today.

But nothing he had witnessed could have prepared Him for this visitation. In Revelation 1:10, John says, "I was in the Spirit on the Lord's Day and heard behind me a great voice, as of a trumpet."

> The voice of the Lord is upon the waters: the God of glory thundereth: the Lord is upon many waters. The voice of the Lord is powerful; the voice of the Lord is full of majesty. The voice of the Lord breaketh the cedars; yea, the Lord breaketh the cedars of Lebanon. He maketh them also to skip like a calf; Lebanon and Sirion like a young unicorn. The voice of the Lord divideth the flames of fire. The voice of the Lord shaketh the wilderness; the Lord shaketh the wilderness of Kadesh. The voice of the Lord maketh the hinds to calve, and discovereth the forests: and in His temple doth every one speak of His glory.
>
> Psalms 29:3–9

When Jesus walked and talked with His disciples, His voice was that of a human being. But now, John is describing His Lord's voice as a "great voice, as of a trumpet."

He had never heard such a voice before.

Imagine: As John was in the filthy living conditions of Patmos, caged and treated like an animal with the common criminals, what must it have been like for him to be startled out of this last place on earth for the doomed, where it appeared his life would end, by the sound of this powerful, ear-splitting voice?

No one else on Patmos heard the sound John heard. The others were not in the Spirit on the Lord's Day! Many sitting around you do not hear the Lord's voice either, for their ears are not tuned to the frequency of Jesus' voice.

John's testimony reveals he was still pursuing the Lord as He always had. But face it: Circumstances sometimes position us with our backs to the Lord. We still worship Him as we have always known Him, but we are not positioned to see where He's standing in the light of our life's situations.

While John's back was still turned away, a message came: "I am the Alpha and Omega, the first and the last" (Revelation 1:8). This is the only place in the Bible where this description is used. Why would Jesus introduce Himself to John in this way? For the same reason He introduced Himself to Moses as "I Am that I Am." Jesus wanted John to know that He preceded everything that was and is, and He will be there when it's all said and done.

We are not the beginning of things and we are not the end; Jesus is!

Just because John sat in a particular and terrible place did not mean that Jesus could not come to Him and reveal Himself as God!

When you are in what you might consider the last place you could ever possibly be, remember this: You are not last; Jesus is!

When you've gone as far as you can go and have seen as far as you can see, there is still Someone greater than you, Someone who is the finality of all things.

When He says, "You are not finished," then you are not yet finished. Some may feel like saying, "This is it, it's over for me"—but has Jesus spoken the last word yet?

John said the voice sounded behind him, causing him to turn from the direction he was facing, towards the voice. So many people are looking backwards to where Jesus used to be. John's thought might have been to muse about the "good old days" that had been wonderful. Maybe he was even reliving those past glorious moments of which he had been a part. Maybe, as he sat in the degradation of humanity, he longed for days gone by. But Jesus would have no part of it…

Jesus spoke and awakened John from his backwards glance at the yesteryears of glory and compelled him to turn and face Him where He was right at that moment—that day. This is a great need of the church today: to get our eyes off the past and face forward to see where Jesus is today, right now, at this moment.

Many people missed the visitation of the Lord as He walked on earth, and many today are missing it because they are still relishing days gone by. Many revivalists are languishing because yesterday's fire has gone out.

A few years ago, the Lord gave me a word for the church—in a single sentence. I saw the revived church of believers standing on a pathway, looking stuck in that spot as they were wondering where all the fire and glory had gone. The Lord said, "I'm not where you were; I'm where you're going. Keep coming." I saw Him beckoning them down the road.

Many times, we want to relive over and over again the highlights of our faith. But by doing so, we miss the new, every-morning side of God. God's people today need to hear, first and foremost, the voice of Jesus sounding up close and personal, in their space of old memories!

So John heard Jesus, but then He also saw Jesus. A woman in a church some years ago came up to me and asked, "Have you ever seen Jesus? I have!" It was a prideful statement of competition, and one that was not backed up by integrity or purity.

So many claim to have seen Jesus or had visions of Him, but can casually talk about it, like they are reporting the evening news. John said in Revelation 1:12, "I turned to see the voice that spoke with me and being turned I saw seven golden candlesticks." We need to understand what John was saying. He turned to see the voice that was speaking with him. The voice of Jesus *is* Jesus; the two are not separated into a voice and a Jesus.

Many people today want Jesus, but they do not want what He says to them. Jesus is the Word of God. He is the Sword. He is the Voice. If you have truly had a vision of Jesus, you will have heard His voice, too—maybe not audibly, but you will know what He has said.

The Bible tells us that "out of the abundance of the heart, the mouth speaks" (Matthew 12:34). We, too, reveal our hearts, which give definition to our actions by what comes out of our mouths: faith or doubt, truth or lies, fear or confidence, love or hatred.

Where did Jesus focus John's attention? On the very thing Jesus set up before He left this earth, the very thing for which He died: the church. John saw why, because the central figure standing in the midst of the seven golden candlesticks was, in John's word, "one like unto the Son of man, clothed with a garment down to the foot and girt about the chest with a golden girdle" (Revelation 1:13).

This is the crux of the whole matter: Jesus and His church!

The woman I mentioned who had "seen Jesus" cared nothing for the church; rather, she was a person of strife and agitation within the church she attended. That is not the heart of Christ towards His church, and anyone with a vision of Jesus sees what Jesus sees.

I am amazed at those who are so mixed up today that they make the church about a denomination, a house church, or sitting home with one's Bible. But Jesus was standing in the midst of seven contemporary churches of John's day, as listed in verse 11, which records exactly what Jesus said to John.

God gave a Word to our church here that brought a mandate upon us to "get our feet in the door of the church and pray," for many were in danger of totally shutting out the Spirit of God from His church. We are in an emergency status today concerning the church, as it parallels the churches of Asia. Reading through the issues Jesus Christ had with these churches is very revealing and should strike the fear of God in the hearts of those called by His Name.

Taking a closer look at Jesus in this first chapter of Revelation, verses 13–16, gives us great insight into this Christ who stood before John. Look at what John saw:

His garment down to His feet—not the garment of the Galilean!

His chest bound about with a golden breastplate—not a soft, blue sash!

His hair white as wool, as white as snow—not brown, wavy hair and trimmed beard!

His eyes as flames of fire—not soft, brown eyes!

His feet like fine brass with the appearance of glowing fire—not dusty, sandaled feet!

His voice the sound of many waters—not the voice of a man!

His right hand holding the seven stars—not the calloused hands of a carpenter!

His mouth with a sharp, two-edged sword coming forth—not a human mouth of human words!

His countenance as bright as the sun shines in its strength—not the sun-beaten face of a traveler along earth's paths!

Oh yes, we love to portray Jesus looking just like He looked as a man walking the earth. We love to retrace His steps along the shores of Galilee. We imagine Him in paintings and note how His eyes are loving and sweet as they look at us.

But to view Christ in frames of His past life is to trap Him in the veil of His flesh. This will cause us to miss Him in the splendor of His glory sitting at His Father's right hand, coming back in power and glory. We must see Him as the Court of Last Resort, the King of Kings, and the Judge of Everything.

We must quit humanizing God!

He is not like us!

We are to be like Him!

John had never seen Jesus like this! No painter can capture the likeness of Christ on canvas. How can you paint truth, righteousness, justice, love, wrath, holiness, fearsomeness, kindness—all with the stroke of a brush?

It takes one who has seen Him to describe Him, and even then, John was limited by human words to let us know that we must see Him for ourselves. John's revelation can only take us so far.

John's response in verse 17, "and when I saw Him, I fell at His feet as dead," tells all! He was overcome with the power of the Holy One standing before him. This Jesus was like no Jesus he had ever met. Before, he could sit at His feet, eat with Him, and follow Him from city to city; now, He could not even stand in His presence. Isaiah understood the feeling:

> I saw also the Lord sitting upon a throne, high and lifted up, and His train filled the temple. Above it stood the seraphims: each one had six wings; with twain He covered His face, and with twain He covered His feet, and with twain He did fly. And one cried unto another, and said, "Holy, holy, holy, is the LORD of hosts: the whole earth is full of His glory." And the posts of the door moved at the voice of him that cried, and the house was filled with smoke. Then said I, "Woe is me! for I am undone; because I am a man of unclean lips, and I dwell in the midst of a people of unclean lips: for mine eyes have seen the King, the LORD of hosts."
>
> ISAIAH 6:1–5

Today, the church is very much alive, standing up tall and strong, and it knows nothing about falling "as one dead" at the feet of Jesus—but you and I should! Today, the church knows nothing about the sharp, double-edged sword of Jesus' mouth—but you and I should!

> For the word of God is quick, and powerful, and sharper than any two-edged sword, piercing even to the dividing asunder of soul and spirit, and of the joints and marrow, and is a discerner of the thoughts and intents of the heart. Neither is there any creature that is not manifest in His sight: but all things are naked and opened unto the eyes of Him with whom we have to do.
>
> HEBREWS 4:12–13

His Word bares our souls! His voice slices to the very core of our matter and reveals our hearts in the brightness of His light. Until we see Jesus in this light, we will know nothing of falling at His feet "as dead" to ourselves. This falling down is indicative of utterly emptying ourselves of all our abilities to stand on our own feet in the presence of Jesus Christ in His glory.

All pride will fall down as dead.

All ideas and concepts about Jesus will fall down and die.

All past revivals will bend and die to the move of Christ towards His church in these Last Days, for what He is about to do outshines them all!

No one will stand up and say, "That isn't God!"

People in past moves of God and even in what He is doing today stumble greatly over God's touch on the human flesh and they collapse under the weight of His glory. People have overanalyzed the power of God until they have made Him impotent in His ability to slay their flesh on any level. On the other hand, people have oversimplified the power of God and have made a game of God touching their physical bodies by looking everywhere for someone to lay hands on them and impart something to them. But what happened to John will have none of any of that. It's not the falling down that we should be excited about, but the encounter with Jesus Christ, who is altogether holy! If you really see and hear Him, you will know—and you, too, will fall as one dead at the feet of Jesus.

John the Baptist was born in a specific, prophetic time during which his whole life was dedicated to preparing the church for Jesus' appearance. Throughout the ages, other messengers in other prophetic times have also prepared the church. Now, about two thousand years after John the Baptist, here we are: messengers who once again are preparing God's people for His appearance.

The only difference between the One who came to John in the Jordan River and the One we see in the book of Revelation is the title: the Lamb and the Lion. He is not revealing Himself to us as the suffering Savior, the Gentle Lamb, or the appealing, soft-spoken God of love. We are encountering the Lion, the Lord of Glory, the Great I Am, the Alpha and Omega, the Beginning and the End, who is and was and is to come, the One seated at the right hand of God, the One who has been making intercession for the saints of God (Romans 8:34) while we have been seeding heaven with our prayers of intercession for souls.

We can have no part in what God is about to do if we don't get the revelation of Christ.

I do not believe people who have trapped Jesus into their religious outlines of how He fits into their lives are going to be ready to meet the Jesus who is coming back to make war with the nations (Revelation 19:11).

We are living in precarious times of war, pestilence, storms, and shakings, with whole nations shifting off long-ago-built foundations. God desires people who truly know Jesus for who He is today, in our world—not only the One He was to us the day we were saved.

Where we are going as believers, we must have a fresh revelation of Christ, the Omega Christ, the Christ of all finalities, the End of all Things! If we don't get this, then we will do the rest of what God has called us to do on yesterday's encounter, finishing in the flesh what was begun in the Spirit.

"Having begun [commenced] in the Spirit, are ye now made perfect [to complete] by the flesh?" (Galatians 3:3b). It is time for a fresh encounter with Jesus.

The reason for the weariness and difficulty of the hour is because the alpha revelation of Christ we had at salvation, the alpha revelation of Christ we had at the beginning of revival, and the midterm revelation of Christ we had last year will not carry us to the prophetic destination without the omega revelation of Christ.

We must have a fresh encounter with the Omega Jesus of the Last Days, the One who finishes what *He* started (2 Corinthians 8:6). He's the One on the scene now—not the Child in the manger, the Jesus on the cross, or the One in the tomb. This Jesus Christ of the now and Jesus Christ of Revelation will finish what He has said He will to utter completion.

> **John 4:34**—"My meat is to do the will of him that sent me, and to finish his work."

> **John 17:4**—"I have finished the work which thou gave me to do."

> **John 19:30b**—"It is finished: and he bowed his head, and gave up the ghost."

We are entering the season of the "Omega Church" because we are getting ready to encounter the Omega Christ, the end of all things.

The omega believers—the omega church of the Last Days—who have a revelation of the Omega Christ of the Last Days will not wait for Jesus to turn over their tables; they will kick them over themselves because they know they must be cast away like religious clutter. They will do this in preparation for the Lord entering His Temple without hindrance.

This omega revelation of Christ will totally undo us, bend us, and break us!

We won't be seeking supernatural powers as the goal of our pursuit because a fresh revelation of the Omega Christ will put it all in perspective. He's the First and the Last; it's all about Him, and all we need is found in Him! No angels or encounters with any other created beings will do for people who have encountered the Omega Christ. No almost-pure, halfway obedient person will have this kind of revelation. It is reserved for those who are in the Spirit on the Lord's Day!

John was visited in this way because He was right where God had placed Him for His glory. How God used him is not how God is going to use you, but to seek Christ for today is something we all must do. Yesterday's visitations will not take us where Jesus is leading His church.

There is an impact from seeing Jesus how He really is—today, now! This encounter leaves people rising up differently than when they went down; they are changed!

There is a Last-Days church, there are believers who will arise to meet the demands of the season, to go ahead and fulfill the mandate, the vision, the prophecy that has been given to them. They will go forth not in their own inspiration, but straight from a holy visitation with Jesus Christ, the King of the first and the last.

This church, this believer, this prophet, this teacher, this preacher, this apostle, this evangelist will rise up in the likeness of Jesus Christ, without spot, wrinkle, or any such thing.

This one will defend truth with his or her life and demolish deception and error at its root.

This one will hunger and thirst after righteousness.

This one will be filled with the Holy Ghost and fire!

This one will love God's Word.

This one will be a seasoned warrior intercessor.

This one will be fearless in the face of opposition.

This one will be a destructive force to the devil's kingdom.

This one will be of one heart, mind, and spirit—singly focused.

This one will not move in doubt, fear, and unbelief.

This one will be a fierce defender of the faith.

This one will have eyes only for Jesus.

This one will carry the banner of Jesus and His shed blood, without shame of His Name.

This one will know the sound of the roar in his or her ears.

And if this one is you, you will be strong, prepared, patient, persevering, godly, filled with faith, have clear vision, possess sharp discernment, know where to tap into wisdom and understanding, and be humble. He will lay His head upon you and say, "Fear not, I am the first and the last. I am He that lives and was dead and behold, I am alive forevermore. Amen. And I have the keys of hell and of death!" (Revelation 1:18).

Are you ready to encounter the One with the keys?

chapter eighteen

The Anchor of Our Faith

Faith is the hand by which we take hold of the Person and work of our Redeemer, Jesus Christ.

Anchor: "A person or thing that can be relied on for support, stability, or security; mainstay: to fix or fasten; affix firmly: A source of security or stability."

Drag anchor (of a vessel): "To move with a current or wind because an anchor has failed to hold."

"If you fear, put all your trust in God: that anchor holds" (Hebrews 6:19). The word "anchor" is used metaphorically for that which supports or keeps one steadfast in time of trial or doubt.

Faith: "Persuasion, moral conviction of religious truth, or the truthfulness of God; fidelity, faithfulness; the character of one who can be relied on; belief that does not rest on logical proof or material evidence."

Our whole faith, the totality of our faith, hinges on whether we believe and trust God in every way, no matter what we see, feel, or experience. Many Christians have selective faith, the kind that works when the road is easy or the task is not too great. There is a faith that is tough, rugged, persevering, and believing. It is a faith that pushes you to believe God, in spite of all the facts, circumstances, and evidence that mounts up to call Him unfair, unreliable, untruthful, or negligent.

This faith hangs on to the only reliable One in the midst of life's many storms and challenges. At this time in history, a head knowledge gained from years of sitting on soft church pews will not suffice. We must believe God to the fullest, possibly in some of the most challenging times of our lives. People have believed and trusted in many things now being shaken…so their confidence is now being shaken.

Even the church and its people have wrongly established their lives and future on the very things God has promised to shake, until the unshakeable will remain. With the times facing us, many people who have been softened by years of soft service, soft living, soft worship, soft prayer, and soft giving are going to find a deficit in the area of faith in God because living by faith is not what they have invested their lives in.

When our security is found in our bank accounts, homes, cars, abilities, positions, and other earthly things, or in denominations, governments, leaders, and other personalities, any shifting from those things that are foundational to many lives will bring ruin to the man-structured Christianity in which many believe. Faith in what we believe and say is not faith at all. True faith is being wholeheartedly committed to what God says and believes. If our faith in His Word and promises is mingled with obedience and an absolute trust in God, we will stand on solid ground when the trials of our faith do occur. God has every right to test our faith, to prove it through fiery trials. This is something people don't appreciate about God—His tests. But, test, He does.

Sometimes, what He asks of us is the biggest test of all, one that tests us to the core of our faith. Having been raised in the home of a pastor who had the heart of a pioneer, a sojourner who traveled according to the call of God, I know that it took *faith* to pull up roots from familiar ground, leave it all behind, and just go...based solely on the Word of God.

I've heard my dad say each time we have "sojourned to a new land" that "God spoke to my heart and told me to go." Well, people can believe and go, or they can rationalize and not go.

There are people who have been uprooted in more than one way. Some have uprooted from stale religion, leaving behind their old comfort zones for the new world of raw faith. Some have uprooted from old mindsets that entrapped them and bound them to the smallness of their own doubt, fear, and unbelief for the new land of faith. Some have uprooted ministries for the higher ground of the glory and power of God being manifested. Some have uprooted and moved to a place of God's calling to be in God's "there" for them.

For whatever reason you feel God has called you to uproot, it takes a bold step...but one filled with great, untested zeal, that which we call faith when we are excited about the venture. How wonderful faith is when it is "the-new-land, we're-moving-out" kind of faith! How dreadful it becomes when we realize we are far removed from our old base and nothing is left to hang on to except God's unchanging, faithful hand. This is where we must come to grips with the fact that, regardless of all other evidence, God's Word is true.

"For when God made a promise to Abraham, because he could swear by no greater, he swore by Himself" (Hebrews 6:13). God gave His Word based on His own Word.

People today are trying to extract from God something besides His Word, to validate God with facts, numbers, and other stats. What He did was give a promise, vow, take an oath that He does not lie. When He swears by Himself, there is none greater, no one higher, no one more committed to His Word than Himself.

There's nothing and no one greater that God can put His right hand upon than His own Word and swear, "What I am saying is the truth, the whole truth, and nothing else but the truth!"

It all boils down to this: Do we believe God or not? Can we trust God? Is His Word a faithful and true Word? Are His promises "Yes and Amen?" Can we have confidence that His blessings, His Word, and His promises will come to pass?

"Saying, Surely blessing I will bless thee, and multiplying I will multiply thee. And so, after he [Abraham] had patiently endured, he obtained the promise" (Hebrews 6:14–15). "After he had patiently endured" is translated from the Hebrew *makrothumeo* (*Strong's* 3114), which means "to be of a long spirit, not to lose heart; to persevere patiently and bravely in enduring misfortunes and troubles." This definition has very powerful implications for us if we are able to do the same thing: Patiently endure = obtain!

This is a major key to faith: to be patient, to wait, to believe God concerning the promise He has given us.

> For men verily swear by the greater: and an oath for confirmation is to them an end of all strife. Wherein God, willing more abundantly [over and above all that is necessary] to show unto the heirs of promise the immutability [unchangeable, fixed, and unalterable] of His counsel, confirmed [to act as a sponsor or a guarantor; to pledge oneself, to give surety] it by an oath [a fence, a limit; i.e., sacred restraint].
>
> HEBREWS 6:16–17

Oath: "A fence, a sacred restraint."

What a beautiful picture for us to consider! God has fenced Himself in with His own Word. That is what an oath is: a sacred restraint.

> That by two immutable [unchangeable, fixed, and unalterable] things, in which it was impossible for God to lie, we might have a strong consolation, who have fled for refuge to lay hold upon the hope set before us.
>
> HEBREWS 6:18

When everything in the world shifts and changes, God's promises, His Word, is…immutable…unchangeable…fixed…unalterable! God will confirm one thing to us: not the details of the promise, but the immutability of His counsel. He has it fixed, unchangeable, unalterable, by His oath, the sacred restraint. He promises, He confirms. I think sometimes we would rather have the details than the confirmation that He keeps His promises.

"Which hope we have as an anchor of the soul, both sure and steadfast [cannot be shaken], and which entered into that within the veil" (Hebrews 6:19). Faith in God is the needed anchor…the anchor is His Word, which was made manifest through and in Jesus Christ.

Many people are slipping and sliding on some very unstable ground—ground that has been made unstable because of disobedience to God on some level.

Jesus said that the ground is turned into *rock* by obedience and *sand* by disobedience.

> Therefore whosoever hears these sayings of mine, and doeth them, I will liken him unto a wise man, which built his house upon a rock: And the rain descended, and the floods came, and the winds blew, and beat upon that house; and it fell not: for it was founded upon a rock. And every one that hears these sayings of mine, and doeth them not, shall be likened unto a foolish man, which built his house upon the sand: And the rain descended, and the floods came, and the winds blew, and beat upon that house; and it fell: and great was the fall of it.
>
> MATTHEW 7:24–27

The world all around us is violently shaking. Just about everything man has placed his confidence in is being shaken. Man is being shaken. The nations are being shaken. The only stable thing right now is God! The only things that remain steadfast and sure are the Word of God and His promises to His children.

The only way *not* to be shaken is to be fixed in the right

place—on the right journey—heading for a city whose builder and maker is God.

> Whose voice then shook the earth: but now He [Jesus] has promised, saying, "Yet once more I shake not the earth only, but also heaven." And this word, "Yet once more," signifies the removing of those things that are shaken, as of things that are made, that those things which cannot be shaken may remain.
>
> HEBREWS 12:26–27

I believe God wants the eyes of His children to focus on eternal matters at this time in history, so He will work to remove every false hope we have in temporal, shallow, earthly things. This is the kind of shaking God did on the rich man who decided in a time of abundance that he would lavish his wealth on himself and live a soft life.

"Whither the forerunner is for us entered, even Jesus, made a high priest for ever after the order of Melchizedek" (Hebrews 6:20).

When Abraham left his homeland comfort zone of normal living, obedient to God by getting up and going, he had to leave everything behind for that which he could not see. All he had were his *faith* and *hope*. That's all we have. If you have been a child of God for any length of time, you know that's all you have—and it's enough to get the job done!

What leaders of the church today need to understand is that the HOPE of the PROMISE is found in being obedient—going where called, even if we don't have all the details of our package when we get there.

Many in the ministry have it backwards today: they try to figure it all out before obeying, instead of having a Word from God first, and then going. God, when in charge of the journey and the promise, will usually give very few details; He'll just tell us to "go."

We not only live in *fast-paced* world, but we also live in a *fact-laced* world, one in which the stats must be printed out on fact sheets for us. Abraham, however, did not ask for the facts. He did not ask what his salary was going to be. He did not ask what his housing package would look like. He didn't ask if he would have medical insurance, Social Security, or a retirement package. He didn't ask for a map, the size of the city, or the number of constituents in the ministry. He simply obeyed. He got up and went, based solely on God's Word, God's oath, to Him—and a hope and a promise.

"By faith Abraham, when he was called to go out into a place which he should after receive for an inheritance, obeyed; and he went out, not knowing whither he went" (Hebrews 11:8). There is a kind of *faith* about which the church of today knows very little. But because of the sojourners of faith, trails have been blazed and churches have been built in lands of promise all over the world.

I know it was not easy for them, no more than it was easy for the pioneers who blazed the trails in the American West to do what they did. They met hardships, opposition, back-breaking work, and difficulties that stretched them beyond what they thought they could bear.

The church today, even the revival church, has a bogus idea that everything is going to be easy; if trouble comes, they quickly lose hope and faint.

Faith moves mountains, blazes trails, opens doors, tears down, and builds up. Faith endures the hardships, the tough times, the persecution, the lack, the fierce winters of the soul. Faith rejoices in the blessings of God and His promise, no matter what the journey looks or feels like.

We look back with respect upon the faith of Abraham, holding him in high regard as someone who believed God and finished his course. We marvel at the remarkable tenacity of the faithful listed in Hebrews 11. There are still multitudes of people who, in the same spirit and heart of the saints of old, continued to get up and go to their "land of promise," just as faithfully as Abraham and the martyrs of Hebrews 11.

Abraham is called "the father of our faith" because he was called to a place he did not know, but went anyway, solely depending on God's Word to him. Because of his obedience to get up and go—to take the journey—he discovered the place of God's greatest promise to mankind: Salem, Jerusalem, Zion, Moriah—what we now know as Israel. And as we know, the devil is trying everything to steal the Promised Land not from the Jews, but from Jesus Christ!

When a land is called a land of promise, it is loaded with the full potential of God to bring forth things that will strike fear in the heart of God's enemy, the devil. That is what all the warfare is about for many of you: You stand on land that is filled with promise, and the devil is afraid that if you take the land, God will prevail, Jesus Christ will have a throne in the hearts of men, and he—the devil—will be evicted.

If you want to know ultimately what God is trying to do with you, read the end of the Book. It's all about the dominating force of God working in you to destroy the works of the devil, to cast him out, to, as it were, with vengeance, trample him under holy feet anointed by God to take the land.

> By faith Abraham, when he was called to go out into a place which he should after receive for an inheritance, obeyed; and he went out, not knowing whither he went. By faith he sojourned in the land of promise, as in a strange country, dwelling in tabernacles with Isaac and Jacob, the heirs with him of the same promise: For he looked for a city which hath foundations, whose builder and maker is God.
>
> HEBREWS 11:8–10

By faith Abraham traveled into the land of promise, dwelling with Isaac and Jacob. Think about it: When he was on this journey, Isaac and Jacob were not yet born. All he had was the promise. But this states he was dwelling in tabernacles with Isaac and Jacob! The Scripture reveals a truth to us: Abraham, because of his faith to get up and go to the land of promise, carried within him the seed of Isaac and Jacob.

Though they were not yet born, Abraham dwelt with Isaac and Jacob by faith. God had given His Word, was bound to His Word, and was fenced in with His Word by His oath, His sacred restraint. Every obedient sojourner is loaded with the promise of God. If you will just get to the place where God has called you, your promise, your Isaac and Jacob will become a reality.

chapter nineteen

Invisible Faith, Elusive Faith

> "Now faith is the substance of things hoped for, the evidence of things not seen.... Through faith we understand that the worlds were framed by the word of God, so that things which are seen were not made of things which do appear."
>
> Hebrews 11:1 and 3

We are living in one of the most challenging times for the people of God and His church as the end times unfurl with all their dynamic changes. In the midst of all that is occurring, God has spoken some very powerful, life-changing truths through His written Word and His prophetic voice.

God has assigned and mandated His people with specific assignments in specific fields of ministry all over the world. This is not about titles or positions, it's about a calling to be there, go forth, or just stand, persevere, and remain fixed, to hold fast our course and finish the race.

God opened a door of opportunity, and many of you stepped

through with great anticipation and passion only to discover "closed places," like a great wall of resistance that stood before you in a face-off. We've all been there, facing a door or doors that we want to enter, but we don't have the key(s).

To be locked out is very frustrating.

I have circled my house looking for any way to get in when the doors have been locked and I haven't had the keys. There's no way to describe the hopeless feeling I have when I know I have a right to be inside, but am stuck outside.

Keys are very important to accessing the places we want to enter.

Key: "Something that affords a means of access: something that secures or controls entrance to a place: A position or condition which affords entrance, control, possession: that which serves to unlock, open, discover, or solve something unknown or difficult."

Keys are frequently mentioned in Scripture. In Hebrew, a "key" is called "the opener" (Judges 3:25); in the Greek New Testament it is called "shutting" (Matthew 16:19; Luke 11:52; Revelation 1:18, etc.). The word is used figuratively for power, authority, or office (Isaiah 22:22; Revelation 1:8 and 3:7; comp. 9:1 and 20:1; comp. also Matthew 16:19 and 18:18).

The Bible talks about keys, revealing that they are very real. But many times, life's circumstances can blind our vision to them or cause us to lose our grip on them.

Invisible things offer us a great challenge because of the lack of physical substance. Look at the following list and see if you have ever physically seen these keys…and yet, they exist!

- The keys of the kingdom of heaven (Matthew 16:19)
- The key of knowledge (Luke 11:52)
- The key of David (Revelation 3:7)
- The key of the bottomless pit (Revelation 20:1)
- The keys of hell and of death (Revelation 1:18)

The keeper of the keys has the power to open and to shut; in the New Testament, the keys denote power and authority of various kinds.

While I understand that the phrase "faith key" is not specifically mentioned in the Bible, the idea behind this message is that it takes faith in Christ to use the keys He's given us to open the doors before us.

Each of you reading this can name the door you personally face, for in each of our lives and ministries, we face a plethora of closed places, places into which we need real breakthrough and unhindered access. It may be within our families, our ministries, our cities, our states, or our nation. Or, it may be hard-to-open, hard-to-access places.

We may call these "doors of opposition" or "doors of opportunity," but the truth is this: opposition and opportunity, many times, are represented by the same door.

There are doors that need to be unlocked, and it will take a "faith key" to unlock them. The frustrating thing about these doors is that, unlike the front door on your house, these cannot be seen…they're something you cannot get a handle on. These doors are in the invisible realm, and the keys are invisible keys. But, if one can get the keys of faith in his or her spiritual hands and actually get the doors open, a wealth of supply that is much needed in the physical realm is inside those doors.

"Now unto the King eternal, immortal, invisible, the only wise God, be honor and glory forever and ever. Amen" (1 Timothy 1:17). It is like this: "invisible faith" for "invisible things" connected to an "invisible God," who has given us only one thing—His Word!

Faith might also be called "elusive faith" because there is absolutely nothing concrete about it. We spend a great deal of our Christian lives trying to get hold of that part of our being in which the Word states that God has given everyone a "measure of faith."

"If I could just get hold of that faith, I know it's there…"

"If I could just get it to work for me here…"

We spend much time trying to find it, track it down, define it, and make it work for us.

When God says, "Such and such things will happen, can happen, and are going to happen," it is up to us to align ourselves, our hearts, and our minds with His Word to believe that He will do what He said, and that He will bring it to pass.

We might be prone to think that what God has asked us to believe is greater, harder, more than, or bigger than what other people have been asked to believe; therefore, we suppose that our journey into faith is much more difficult than that of others.

The reason for this is that each of us is on a very unique, individual journey, replete with our own circumstances, problems, difficulties, and losses. Add to that—besides the things that arise to buffet us on the journey—we also are moved to believe God will answer prayer and meet our needs and those of others. We are moved to believe God's Word and take it at face value, that the God we read about is really interested in the things that come into our lives.

If we look at God's Word, at people in the Word, and even at revivalist, church, and missions history, we will see that God has always asked His people to believe something too hard, too big, too long, and too far-fetched. In other words, He has always asked His people to believe for the impossible!

Look at these, just to name a few:

Noah was chosen by God to stand in the gap for the earth. He was the last in the line of godliness in a totally corrupted world (see Genesis 6:11–13). And we think we have it bad? Noah wasn't even given hope that he would see anyone saved. He wasn't promised church growth. It was going to be a lonely trip for this man and his family!

Moses was called by God to take a stand under some very difficult circumstances (see Exodus 2:11; 3:2–4, 10–11). It was not easy doing what God called him to do. He had some very hard choices to make because he was called to stand in the gap for his kinsmen. Doing so would make him an enemy of the system under which he had been raised, but he chose to identify with God and His people. Because of God's call on his life, he was about to be stretched way beyond his comfort zone.

Joshua was commissioned to destroy every trace of sin in Canaan by tearing down the Canaanites' altars, images, and groves (see Joshua 1:2). He would come up against idolatry, witchcraft, and the floods of spirits that used those doors to gain entrance. He would see the wages of sin in the citizens of his region, and maybe even at times he felt powerless to stem the tide of ungodliness.

Gideon was a man to whom God sent an angel (Judges 6:12). He was from a family line deeply entrenched in idolatry. He was instructed to make a sacrifice and tear down the idols of his family. He was called a mighty man of valor, which in and of itself was a shocking title, considering the condition in which he was found. What was said to Gideon was that he had it in him to rise up to the occasion God was calling him to. The numbers Gideon was given to deal with, though they didn't make sense according to military thinking, added up to victory as he stepped into a humanly impossible situation.

God always asks His people to believe in what they cannot personally achieve. Think of the missionaries who have stood on foreign soil, ready to declare the gospel to a needy people. Think of pastors who have entered cities to plant churches and reach the lost. Think of revivalists who have stood against the deepening tide of apathy and worldliness in the church, and of the intercessors who have entered the field of battle armed only with prayer as they faced godless landscapes. And think of the souls who have stood alone in hard places, separated from others by time and vision.

Many of you are currently standing in a difficult place. You might be at a crossroads or getting ready to turn a corner around which you don't know what you'll find…but you know in your heart that you are where you are supposed to be.

Many people have been called into the missions field and have stood for years seeing no salvations. Many have even died without seeing the promises come to pass; yet they have remained faithful because God said to do it.

Sometimes that is all we need: to just do it because God said "do it." The hard work of obedience tills up our hard ground into soft soil.

chapter twenty

We Do Not Live by Sight

> "For we walk by faith, not by sight."
>
> 2 Corinthians 5:7

We are very tactile, sensory people, discerning our world by our senses. We lean almost completely on what we can see, touch, taste, smell, and hear—and on what we know to be. We live most of our lives in the comfort of that zone.

If we can make it happen, see it happen, feel it happen, hear it happen, smell it, be in charge of the outcome, and feel like we had a part in it, we are satisfied. We are controlled by our senses.

Faith is a realm in which we have to move beyond our senses. God wants to raise His church up not to be led solely by sights, sounds, smells, and what we know to be within our concrete world of our mindsets of church and family life.

While we live in a very real world where we touch and see, faith is "floating," uncontrolled by our natural senses yet attached deep within our hearts to the only thing solid in the faith world: God and His unfailing Word.

We read the phrases "through faith" and "by faith" in Hebrews 11. These noble souls who served their Lord under some very adverse circumstances had found the secret to the reservoir of faith somewhere deep inside their innermost beings. They were able to draw strength, focus, and power through and by faith as they walked through great difficulty, adversity, and persecution.

We live in a time of "easy believism," a kind of religion that was foreign to these people who embraced the promises of God and lived on the cutting edge of His Word, walking out each challenging step of their faith in obedient confidence, knowing that God is faithful to His Word! We may tend to immortalize these heroes of faith in a category quite different from ours, feeling as if they reached an apex of faith that we have not found.

I believe that many today—yes, you—are not all that far removed from what kept these people true to God from the inception of their faith until their deaths. Their faith in Christ was the sustaining anchor of their souls, keeping them in the most adverse of circumstances. Multitudes are standing in the face of hatred, prejudice, persecution, and mockery, and yet they stand; they do not waver or recant. They (you) would rather die than forsake their (your) Lord and Savior, Jesus Christ.

Many of God's living faithful have walked and even now are walking out their faith in some very difficult places, feeling as if they are barely making it yet living an overcoming life: denying sin and compromise and conforming their will to the Father's.

Anyone who perseveres exhibits faith.

Anyone who overcomes shows faith.

Faith still ticks deep within our spirits, not birthed or killed by our emotions, mindsets, or human desires. Faith transcends our flesh and lifts us up. Even when our feet are bound by the stocks in some deep prison, faith worships.

We need to stop here and understand that human beings, in any generation of believers, are alike. We are bound by "like precious faith."

Their kind of faith is actually resident in us as well. We have been given the access, the authority, and the power to enter into all Christ did when He walked upon this earth in bodily form. He gave us the keys to the Kingdom (see Matthew 16:19).

These keys are ancient keys, handed down from heaven to earth, placed into the hands of the church by Jesus Christ Himself. They are eternally fastened upon an unending ring of heaven-authorized access. They give authority to enter doors, shut doors, bind, and loosen. They give access to the throne of God and all that is stored up there. They give access to the power and authority that heaven invested in the church through the Holy Spirit's empowerment. They are keys of salvation, healing, and deliverance for the hungry and hurting masses of humanity on this planet.

These keys are the gospel of Jesus Christ, used each time the eyes of spiritual blindness are opened. They are the keys to the Kingdom of God, implemented through intercession. They unlock the darkened minds and spirits of people and release a healing forgiveness through Jesus Christ to many a weary soul who has walked his or her whole life with the weight of guilt and sin. They lock the doors against the enemy's return into lives that are rescued by the grace of God.

They set people free and bind devils.

You, like others who have gone before you, have a chance to walk in the strength and authority granted by God!

You do have the keys. These keys are truth that will free us from ourselves and our limitations, causing our spirits to soar, even though our natural man is earthbound.

These spiritual truth keys, correctly applied, will bring a release to us—not only in our minds, but into deeper places where lasting, life-changing decisions are made.

Part VI

The Keys

"The natural realm is deceptive in that
it produces convincing evidence that influences
and sways us by the power of our senses."

—Esther Dummer

Key 1

Believe God

> "For what saith the scripture?
> Abraham believed God, and it was counted
> unto him for righteousness."
>
> Romans 4:3

These are the foundational facts:

Abraham believed God.

He had to believe God called him out of Ur.

He had to believe God sent him.

He had to believe God knew the way to the end of the journey.

He had to believe God was going to make nations from his seed.

He had to believe God would take Sarah's life and his—old lives and bodies—and birth the purposes of God, giving them a son of promise.

How easy it is for us to believe God for Sarah, in her old age, retirement years, to become pregnant. This is a woman who had never given birth because her womb was dead, yet the story reads quite well to us—as long as it is not us God is asking to believe in something this far-fetched.

Abraham was called upon by God to believe that his wife's dead womb would be opened and that she would bear a child of destiny in her old-age years and that he, as an old man, would be a father of nations.

We need to realize that these people were real, just like us. They were called upon to believe in something "way out there," far removed from the norm. For Abraham to believe God, it took an incredible kind of faith, something that withstood the test of the time that it was going to take for its fulfillment.

Abraham was not told how long or how far into the future this incredible event would happen.

Time does test our faith.

Just like Abraham, you have received a promise filled with prophetic destiny and purpose, and you received no clues from God as to how long the fulfillment of that promise was going to take. This is what has tripped up more people in their faith journey: the time and distance one has plodded along without seeing the end of the road.

How easy it is to look back and dissect someone else's faith! We can, in retrospect, take a look at Abraham's faith under the biblical microscope, but we must remember that he was a mere human being, just like we are. He was asked to go on a journey, he received no road map, and did not know his destination. God simply told him to walk, and said that when he got there, He would let him know.

That is much like us today on our journey with the Lord. Many of God's people in this revival have been on a journey for a good number of years, walking by faith into what God has promised. We can have faith that God will let us know when we have arrived. "Meanwhile, keep walking, just keep going, don't stop, don't take any detours, and just keep going straight ahead on the path I've placed you on," God says. "Until you hear me say something new, keep doing the last thing I said to do, going in the direction that I have led you to step into."

So Abraham journeyed and had a word from God about a "great nation coming from Him." He had no idea how that was to come about, but he believed God. For people to walk into the future without a map or the means to fulfill the promise of God for them, it takes faith.

Key 2

Call It

> "(As it is written, I have made thee a father of many nations,) before him whom he believed, even God, who quickeneth the dead, and calleth those things which be not as though they were."
>
> ROMANS 4:17

The fact is, "those things that are not" don't exist. We can't see them. We can't touch them. The "things that are not" have no physical form, no real valuation, because they simply do not exist at the moment in any form we can see or grasp as a reality.

"Those things that are not" cannot be calculated, tabulated, formulated, or estimated in any natural sense.

Abraham took all those nonexistent things and called them as though they were, in the same way God gave the Word. What exactly does that mean—to "call them as though they were"? Abraham began to speak a word, God's Word, into the space these things would fill, just as God spoke things into existence and hung the worlds upon nothing. God said it was, so it was. When God says a Word, and we speak that Word, it is as though it were a space filled and inhabited by what God said would be there.

When Abraham said, "I am a father of many nations," he was not a father of anything. He was speaking faith words from the space where faith lived, deep within his heart and spirit. It did not matter what his mind calculated about that seeming vacuum; to Abraham, he was already a father.

We must be reminded that Abraham was no angel, but a mortal man who had taken hold of something so far outside of himself that only God could do it. He did not live in a futuristic world like we do so often while waiting and wondering where the promise of the harvest, the healing, or our loved ones' salvation are, but he lived in the "now" Word of God.

Evidently, Abraham had spoken about this coming child often enough that Sarah got the message that her husband really believed in this promised son. During the time when he was calling those things that were not as though they were, Sarah came up barren time and time again.

This is the case with many revivalists in some hard, little places of promise. The womb still feels empty even though the promise has been given that new life is coming. When Abraham told Sarah that she was going to have a child, she suddenly felt responsible to fulfill his expectations of her: have a baby. When God speaks to us of a great harvest coming in, we suddenly feel responsible to fulfill His expectations of giving birth to that great harvest.

But what happens when the womb is still empty?

Sarah's faith wavered. She was not pregnant. She was still an old woman with a dead womb. Eventually, she became frustrated enough that she resorted to self-help. This is a move many people make. We may resort to the old patterns and try to put some things in place to help the vision along, to try to facilitate what God is going to do. But in the process, we actually end up replacing His plan with our own vision of how the promise should come to pass.

Sarah had heard it long enough, and she tried to "manufacture" the son by offering Abraham her handmaiden, Hagar, thinking her child could come from that woman. In Sarah's unbelief, she also influenced the faith of her husband to waver, and he succumbed to the temptation to "make it happen."

We can rationalize just about anything and make it sound so good that we convince ourselves and others that it is "approved by God." After all, we mean well in our service to Him. Then our unbelief ripples out. It is never contained in just one place, but carries influence once it becomes a spoken word of doubt.

Sarah's action circumvented God's plan for her life—temporarily. (Thank God for second chances.) She did not believe in her own womb, and Abraham, for a season, did not believe in her womb.

That's how some of you feel towards your ministry. You may even be looking for a new space where God can move His purpose. You have been sowing the seed of God's Word, but the womb appears dead and does not seem to be accepting this seed. The womb even seems to reject the seed time and time again.

The minute you get your eyes on the "facts," God's Word is silenced by their shout.

Be very careful and discerning during any time of discouragement. If God spoke His Word over that womb, then believe God. Sarah had the promised seed planted into a foreign womb, one she felt was able to give birth to her son.

Folks, there are no surrogate mothers to the thing God is bringing to pass in the womb of promise.

No one else can carry to term what God has said you will carry and give birth to.

There may be other "mothers" who can carry the baby, but it will not be your child.

It is imperative that we do not get ahead of God's timing, no matter how barren we feel.

I ask you today: What is it that God has said you should be saying?

Are we saying the facts as we perceive them, or what God says?

Are we seeing with our eyes, or are we saying what God sees?

"For we walk by faith, not by sight [the external or outward appearance, form figure, shape]" (2 Corinthians 5:7). It is a real challenge to speak "God words" when nothing is yet tangible or visible as evidence. Abraham just said what God said, and within that, he was accurate, right on time, and on target.

It's a real challenge to speak "God words" when the things we perceive by our natural senses and the visible facts tell us something different. Some people think you are crazy because you have been saying what God has said to you for a long time now. You have been speaking it.

I am telling you, the Word of God is sure and true, and what He has said to you is coming, no matter how big or humanly impossible. If you have believed God for revival for your city, for the harvest to come in, for your body to be healed, for signs, for wonders to follow you to confirm the Word of God, then you are within the range of faith becoming sight.

All that God prophesies to us is within the Word of God, prophetically placed in the sequence of God's plan. Your part in that is decreed by the prophetic Word God has given you. You know it is significant to what God is doing, but there is no evidence yet. You must learn to keep speaking the truth.

Decree the decree. Prophesy the prophecy. Sing the new song filled with the sounds of heaven-size faith. God is sending revival to the church. He is sending fresh fire from His altar upon those who have tarried. God is healing His church. God is preparing cities and nations for a great ingathering of harvest power, with the release of signs, wonders, and miracles.

God is preparing us for an Isaiah 61 and Luke 4 ministry of touching the lives of people in deep bondage and pain. He is, even now, placing the harvest sickle in the hands of the prepared church, the people of God who have stood in the hard place, who have endured the time and distance, and who have kept building altars and worshipping God.

God is raising up an army of prayer warriors who will shake the gates of hell. He is sending revival to our youth and children, resulting in a torrent of young people with raw faith being released on whole regions. God is saving whole families. He is calling to the backsliders and the prodigal sons and daughters.

We have been saying these things for years because that is what God has told us to believe, so we speak the "God word," saying what God has said in promise rather than what we see.

It does not matter that these things do not appear to be happening. It does not matter what our eyes see or our ears hear if God has given us a prophetic promise. Saying, seeing, and believing what God says is faith.

Yes, the womb still feels empty; there is no sign of movement or life yet. However, "the vision is yet for an appointed time, but at the end it shall speak, and not lie: though it tarry, wait for it; because it will surely come, it will not tarry" (Habakkuk 2:3).

Once the word is implanted in our hearts, faith builds in direct proportion to how deep it is planted by our own voice of decree.

Key 3

Believe in Hope

> "Who against hope believed in hope,
> that he might become the father of many nations,
> according to that which was spoken,
> So shall thy seed be."
>
> ROMANS 4:18

Most of the church world is more "wishful," as in:
"Oh, I hope it happens."
"I hope God does this."
"I hope my family gets saved."
"I hope my church gets revival."

This is a "Thomas kind of faith," wanting to believe, but having to be convinced in the flesh in order to believe in the spirit. Jesus said in John 20:29, "Thomas, because thou hast seen me, thou hast believed: blessed are they that have not seen, and yet have believed." Within ourselves is the part of us that demands tangible evidence, and yes, sometimes we, like Thomas, find ourselves wanting to put our fingers in the tangible to test the spiritual, to see if it's true. Jesus didn't condemn Thomas for his lack of faith, but He did challenge him to move beyond having to be convinced by some level of proof. We, like Thomas, find ourselves, after the fact, falling on our faces before Jesus and declaring His faithfulness to His Word. How much more blessed we would be if only we could declare it and believe it without having to feel it.

Many believers have found themselves, in a certain time of their lives, wishing for some evidence that God is true to His Word. The natural evidence declares the hopelessness of a situation, but deep inside, we desperately hang on to the intangible things called "promise," "answer," or "breakthrough."

We all want to believe miracles are coming, and that the impossible is going to happen. We want to believe that the thing that seems so far beyond answers is going to break upon us like a refreshing tide of glory. Yet the natural realm grips our hearts and shouts to our senses, "It's not happening!"

God does understand, but He is compelling us to a higher level where our hands do not have to be touching substance to believe.

The words "who against hope believed in hope" make me think of a fortress, a stronghold of faith. Abraham was a man of inner strength built up through prayer and worship. He had grown into a man who believed God's Word to him was true.

Thank God for His grace in allowing each of us time to mature in this area of Christian life. We once were babies, but are now taking some sturdy steps towards the Father's outstretched hands. He beckons, "Come on, walk to Daddy. You can do it."

Abraham developed a stronghold of faith rather than a stronghold of doubt, and he stood fast in what God had said to him. The word "hope" is a noun, not an action on our part.

Abraham believed so that he could become what God had said he would become and do what God said he would do. When he expressed that he was going to be the father of many nations, he was expressing it according to the Word of God; it was not a wish or an "I-hope-so" mentality. He built his strength by hoping in hope, by placing his confidence and trust in what God had said.

For this level of hope, the power of…

…all "maybes" has to be removed.

…all wishful thinking has to be erased and cast down.

…all doubt has to be repented of.

…all fear has to be rebuked and cast out.

God does not lie. He performs all that He says He will. Looking back on Abraham after God performed all He said He would do in Abraham's life is easy. History is always an easy read, but when God asks us to "make history," it's another thing.

So…what has He asked you to do, to believe Him for?

It is our turn now to be the Abrahams of our day and believe God, call those things that are not as though they were, and build a stronghold in hope, believing that God will do what He says He will in our families, churches, cities, harvest fields, and our own bodies.

All the odds were against Abraham. Maybe you feel just like that today.

Everything that could be imagined was there to work against him. His wife's age and her dead womb, his own age, and even his background were unalterable facts. The couple was too old, too far removed from being able to bear any child of promise. The physical evidence said that what God told him was impossible.

Key 4

Be Not Weak in Faith

"And being not weak in faith…"

ROMANS 4:19

When I read this, I see a champion entering the ring, exercised through training, prepared for the victory. We know that a champion doesn't just get up one day and ripple with muscles, but contends for the condition of his body so that he may defeat his foe and win for his side.

How did Abraham build strong faith?

When he left Ur and started on the long journey God had called him to, he began his daily exercise pattern. He began to build altars and worship God.

This was his lifestyle: to offer sacrifice to the Lord in worship. This is the spiritual training ground for faith.

If there is weakness in faith, check the condition of the altar and the depth of the worship that occurs there. Check how often the altar is laid and how deep the worship goes.

Strong faith is in direct proportion to strong worship.

You know what I am talking about. You know that your strength is built at an altar and in worship. You have felt your faith soar to the heavens as you stood before the throne of God in worship. You have stood in corporate worship—and yes, even in time of devotion you have worshipped. In those times, you can believe for anything; that's how powerful worship is. It is a direct line to the throne, and if you make contact, God is big and powerful in that hour.

You have also experienced times when you have struggled to make contact, when you have slacked off in your devotional time with God, or when you have withdrawn from Him in gloom… and have felt the weakness in your spirit settling in. Soon, you become lackluster in your passion for the things of God. Your faith to believe God for anything atrophies and shrivels as quickly as your worship dries up.

I don't think Abraham knew what "many nations" would look like. We can only speculate what the end of our journey will look like. But we have to keep our faith strong through worship to see the journey through.

Abraham was in constant training for the reality to come. His faith rippled with muscles even when his body was old and frail with age, even when he did not see the "body" of evidence to prove beforehand what God had said was true.

How many times do we fail to exercise our faith, keeping it buff with hope, confidence, and trust, and strengthened with our devotional time with God and worship? God wants us to have spiritual muscles as champions of faith contending for breakthrough in the "ring of doubt." When God asks us to believe, we are going to face doubt. We will not escape our minds, but we can defeat our minds and the doubt that resides there.

We are going to have to hit that doubt dead-on with a knock-out blow to the head.

The ring of doubt is the human mind.

> For though we walk in the flesh, we do not war after the flesh: (For the weapons of our warfare are not carnal, but mighty through God to the pulling down of strongholds), Casting down imaginations, and every high thing that exalteth itself against the knowledge of God, and bringing into captivity every thought to the obedience of Christ; And having in a readiness to revenge all disobedience, when your obedience is fulfilled.
>
> 2 Corinthians 10:3–6

Trying to run from doubt is a mind exercise. Our mind is with us. We can't remove our heads and run around without our minds, but neither can we allow our minds to get into the practice of making themselves strong by allowing them to try to figure everything out before we believe in God's Word.

We have opportunity, every time doubt arises in our minds, to pin it to the mat and refuse it the strength or power over us to pin our faith to the mat. We need to cast doubt down and tell it, "You're not speaking into this issue between me and God. You are not a party to our covenant."

You must not give "doubt" a voice.

Some things need to lose their voices. Are you ready for fear to lose its voice? Are you ready for unbelief to lose its voice? Are you ready for doubt to lose its voice? Are you ready for your mind to lose its voice, to quit self-speaking?

We need to stop giving significance to these voices and stop considering them in our application of God's Word to our lives, families, churches, and harvest fields. It is still a mystery to me that, in spite of the fact that Jesus is uttering His voice as the Lion of the Tribe of Judah, releasing a roar over the nations, that I can still be so loud that I cannot hear Him when I am faced with my obstacle, my mountain. These "loudmouths" need to be silenced so that God's voice can be heard and faith can soar into the heavenlies.

Say with me, "I am ready to hear the Word of the Lord, loud and clear!"

Only God has a voice (Psalms 29), and our minds need to be exercised in obedience to understand this truth.

Only God has a voice concerning my church.

Only God has a voice concerning my city.

Only God has a voice concerning my family.

Only God has a voice concerning what He says we will and can do in the Name of Jesus.

Only God has a voice concerning my body.

I can't give doubt a voice, and neither should you. Do not empower it to destroy faith's strength. Worship your way to spiritual vitality, and faith will contend and win every time.

I know we have all felt the wrestling match between faith and doubt. We want to believe, but our minds really raise a hundred arguments. These can be tough times, but we have to remember that faith is not a mind issue; it's a spirit issue.

Doubt issues from the mind and faith issues from the spirit. Every time faith tries to rise up, doubt tries to press it back down into the inner recesses of our being. If our minds can keep control over the issues, then we can explain anything, even defeat. We have to realize that no matter what our mind tells us, faith rules our spirit.

When doubt is strong, the mind rules. When faith is strong, the spirit rules. Faith is a deep, deep sense of knowing where we believe in God's Word to us, in something so great and so far removed from our mind, abilities, and commodities that we cannot even see, touch, taste, smell, or hear it. It is so big and so great that we cannot capture and make it happen in and of ourselves or be visible to our natural senses.

Only God's voice counts in things of faith.

Key 5

Consider Not

> "…he considered not his own body now dead,
> when he was about an hundred years old,
> neither yet the deadness of Sarah's womb."
>
> ROMANS 4:19B

I love this key: "He considered not"! What was it that he gave no consideration to?

He didn't consider his own body or age. He didn't consider the deadness of Sarah's womb. This is where what we see, hear, smell, taste, and touch becomes irrelevant. The things we "see" in the natural are absolutely irrelevant to God's performance of His Word.

I heard God speak to my heart here, "Do not factor the natural evidence into faith."

These are not a part of God's sight.

They're not a part of His vision.

They're not a part of what He's speaking.

These things, the visible, are what the natural mind of man wants to focus on, but there comes a time when we must not factor in the natural at all.

If Abraham and Sarah had owned a full-length mirror, they would have seen with the natural eye an old man and an old woman who were expected to bear the child of promise.

Abraham was one hundred years old, and Sarah had been barren all her life, living with a dead womb. If God wasn't so serious, it could have been laughable! Can you imagine Abraham coming into Sarah month after month, saying, "Sarah, are you with child yet?" She had to say, month after month, "No, Abraham, I am still barren." A monthly look in the mirror would have confirmed what she knew in her head: she was old and barren, and nothing was happening. In fact, nothing was likely to happen in such a dead place.

This was a time in the couple's lives when the natural evidence that preexisted God's Word to them and the continuing evidence of barrenness could not be considered at all. Abraham refused to consider either of them as evidence that God could not do it through them. If he had focused on that, he would have had all he needed to doubt the Word of God because his sight revealed a hopeless mountain of evidence against any movement of God in that womb.

This is what I heard God tell me concerning faith:

Nothing solid counts.

Nothing visible counts.

Nothing real counts.

Nothing dead counts.

You cannot factor in what you can see with your eyes. None of this is a part of the equation. None of this counts to faith. It doesn't matter what you see, think, or feel. That has no bearing whatsoever on God's Word.

God knew the condition into which He was speaking His Word.

He knows when something is barren.

He knows when something is old.

He knows when something is dead and hopeless.

He knows what He's speaking into.

He knew what your situation was when He gave you that Word, called you to walk that path, enter that field, climb that mountain, or face that giant.

He knew what your family, your marriage, your church, your city, your circumstances, your finances, your ministry, and your health was like when He spoke His Word. That is the whole point of God's Word and your faith: to put something into effect that is currently not present or visible, and to change the obvious facts as they now stand to obsolete and God's Word to visible, bringing to sight what He has promised.

What's a hundred-year-old man supposed to do when God tells him that, in spite of the fact that he is old and his wife is barren, "I am going to make you a father of many nations?"

Abraham had only two choices: either move in doubt or move in faith. He chose to believe in God and learned to disregard the mountain of evidence that stood against him in the natural.

Key 6

Don't Stagger

> "He staggered not at the promise
> of God through unbelief…"
>
> ROMANS 4:20A

Doubt and unbelief are paralyzing elements, neutralizing our faith in its tracks. It takes only a pebble of doubt to cause us to stumble.

I don't know how many times the facts, the things that we see, hear, or know, trip us up. If we believe for our healing, what trips us up? A physical manifestation that grips our bodies, the opposing words of our own self-speaking or another's words!

If we believe for provision, what trips us up? The empty bank account, the red in the ledger, the pile of bills, and the calls from collectors.

If we believe for our lost loved ones' salvation, what trips us up? The fact that they still live in rebellion to God, are dysfunctional within the family, and exhibit godless behavior—seemingly far from God's love, grace, and mercy.

If we believe God is going to save our city, what trips us up? The sight of drunks, corruption, dead churches, drugs, and alcohol abuse—the city's strongholds.

Abraham somehow took hold of faith in a way that brought about tenacity—a grip, as it were, on the way God said it was to be. I have seen my father do the same thing as a pastor who blazed a trail in one of America's hottest deserts.

I saw "staggering" in two ways:

- Staggering backwards in unbelief, like "this is way over the top!"
- Walking forward and tripping over the obvious.

We believe more in the facts and the physical evidence of what we can see than we believe God. We can believe more in what our bodies say than in the healing Word of God. We can believe more in the money we make than we can in God's provision when money is not there.

Abraham called those things that are not as though they were and refused to consider the obvious limitations and obstacles as relevant to the fulfillment of God's word. We, likewise, must not stagger at the size of the promise God has given us.

Maybe it's time for us to look in our full-length mirrors and say, "Body, I don't care what you're telling me, what you speak, or what my mind speaks; I'm telling you what God has said. You will line up with the Word of God and be healed in the Name of Jesus." Although my body is saying this or that to me, I will not stagger at the promise of God through unbelief.

This is not a mind game we are playing. It is not mind over matter. It is faith exercised, focused, and enacted to take control of our minds, hearts, and bodies. We cannot be astonished by the magnitude of what God is telling us, and we must not trip over the promise as if it were our barricade to victory. God never gives a promise that cannot reach full maturity.

We should never stagger in unbelief at the size of the promise God has given us.

There may be times when our minds are overwhelmed at what God has asked us to believe in the midst of the mountain of physical evidence that appears to prove why this should not happen. We are really in a fix if the evidence trips us up and then we turn around and the promise finishes us off because it also it too big.

Abraham knew unbelief could beat faith if he contemplated the mountain of evidence that stood in his way or staggered at the size of the promise.

Go ahead, line up everything you can think of in the natural—sick bodies, dead churches, tough towns, broken families, strongholds—and contemplate them long enough as being too much, too big, or taking too long, and doubt will beat faith.

Then line up the spiritual—the prophetic Word of God and the written Word of God and what they tell us we can do, can be, and are—and contemplate it long enough as too big, too much, too hard, or too far, and doubt will beat faith.

If God has revealed one truth to me, it is this: Whether it is the mountainous strongholds of the enemy or the mountainous strength of God's promise, if we consider either one to be too big, we lose.

The enemy would love for us to look at the promise of God and trip, stagger in unbelief, fall on our faces, and admit to defeat, saying, "What God said I could have was just too big, too much, and too far out there for me." He would rather you trip over that than over the size of the mountain; that way, God appears to be the One who "didn't come through."

The enemy would love for us to blame God for why things are not happening as He said. But considering that most of us are not tripping over the promise, the next best thing is for the enemy to make the natural mountain bigger than life—insurmountable. If we contemplate the mountain long enough, we will believe in the mountain to the exclusion of the Word of God and His promises.

But the truth is the enemy and our minds will take either occasion to accuse us and tell us what failures we are. For this reason, we need to worship and put some muscles on our faith to believe God. More of that in a moment…

We need to believe God when nothing is yet in the womb. You, like Abraham, may be looking at Sarah's barrenness and be "calling those things that are not as though they were." Faith, incredible faith!

Abraham had to go through a season of his life declaring, "We are having a baby"— before there was even a pregnancy.

Key 7

Glorify God

"...but was strong in faith, giving glory to God."

Romans 4:20b

The Lord spoke clearly to me that "this is the key to the keys." Think about that statement. We all know that keys unlock doors, but there is a key that releases keys in the spirit and this is it: Give glory to God! When we glorify God, faith grows in strength.

As long as worship is strong and filled with the prophetic decrees of God's promise, faith soars and we can believe God for anything. This is how God has been building our faith and keeping us strong in our faith: worship! Something extraordinary is going on in worship in this move of God. It is not only about the new songs, but about the new sound.

Our voices have become trumpets announcing that Jesus rules and reigns on high.

Our hands and feet become vital and alive as we tread and dance before our King.

The Word of God in our mouths becomes the sword that destroys every enemy of the promise of God in our lives, churches, families, cities, and nations.

Our worship has been a cry and release of our faith in God.

So much of the time, we sing, shout, prophesy, and speak what we believe God has spoken to us over and over, until our faith lifts us up above the mountains of evidence on earth.

Worship releases us from the earthbound place of old mindsets and shackles of religious strongholds that have enveloped the church. When one is seated in the heavenly places with Christ, what devil, stronghold, or circumstance can meet us there? Fear, doubt, and unbelief are left far below as we ascend God's holy mountain.

The lies of the enemy cannot reach our ears when we worship in spirit and truth. We blend intercession for our families, the nations, the harvest, and the church into worship and know beyond a shadow of a doubt that God is going to do it! There is no time that my faith rises to a new level more than when the worship is filled with promise, hope, and faith in God. It is more than singing; it is prophesying what God has said to us. And when it comes back into our ears, we believe!

When there is an anointing on worship, then something uncommon begins to happen. What cannot happen in the flesh begins to form in the spirit. God gets involved with His Word.

When worship, prophecy, intercession, and the anointing remain cohesive and begin to flow as a mighty river of sounds, God moves on behalf of His people. He releases the angelic host to battle. He will release His own voice within the anointed worship as fresh revelation flows from the vessels of worship. The window of heaven will open, and visions will be released as prophetic worship and intercession begin to take place. The glory of God will begin to settle into our midst, and we will become acutely aware of how awesome our God is.

Because of all this heavenly release, worship goes to a new level and becomes all about this great, powerful, and glorious God we serve.

We know nothing on earth or in hell can stop what He says He is going to do among us, in us, and through us. Decrees intensify and the Word becomes alive and moves deep within our hearts.

You're the Lion of the Tribe of Judah!
You have released your roar and the nations shall hear it!
You're my strong tower!
You're the Lord of Hosts!
You are my victory!
You are the salvation to my families and city!
You are the provider of all our needs!
You are my healer!
You are marching upon the land!
You are the reviver!

I don't know what Abraham said to God, but I am sure that it pertained to the greatness of the God he served as he gave glory to God. If Abraham had not built his life on worship and prayer, he would have had a weak faith that would not have allowed him to believe God. No doubt he, like us, spoke back to God the promise of the son and gave God the glory, even before it was within his vision.

Faith grows strong when we speak back to heaven what God released to us from His throne. We must release those words of truth, destiny, promise, and birth, God's Word, and then we hear and believe what we are saying as we become our own prophet and teacher of truth.

God loves His Word being spoken back to Him with faith and worship interwoven into a beautiful tapestry of sound. That's why giving glory to God is so important. Our hearts soar with faith, and we declare, "God, you're going to do it!"

I can feel it to the very core of my being that I am not just speaking vain words here; this is a reality. This is more real than what I can see.

"I don't care what my city, family, or church looks like, God says He is going to save, heal, and deliver—and He's going to use me to do it." This kind of faith happens in worship more than any other place, so we ought to worship all the more.

Worship at home.

Worship in the car.

Worship while shopping.

Worship while at work.

Worship on Monday through Saturday. Worship in the sanctuary. Worship God! Give Him the glory!

Build your altars all along your pathway as Abraham did, giving God the glory and worshipping Him, and your faith will grow and be strong all the time—not just when you are having a good time of worship on Sunday morning.

When Paul and Silas were in jail, having been beaten and placed in stocks, they praised the Lord. When your circumstances, your body, or any other thing in the natural becomes your prison, why not build an altar? Why not prophesy? Why not sing a new song, make a new sound? Why not speak God's Word in faith and believe Him? Why not speak those things that are not as though they were?

I desire for individual faith to become strong, which will make for a very powerful church released on the harvest field. It is not enough for a worship leader to prepare the altar, decree the Word, and prophesy the promise. We need to become faith-bound spiritual sons or daughters of God who will believe God when we are away from our spiritual families. When the devil knocks at the doors of our physical bodies or our homes with his faulty, lying word, why not tell him, "That is not what God said"?

Refuse to believe the evidence of what the enemy tries to pile up against you to create a stronghold of doubt in God's Word. Refuse to consider the evidence, and give God the glory!

By the time Sarah announced she was with child, I believe Abraham said, "I knew it! God said it! Praise God!"

I believe that's how it's going to be with us. We are going to start seeing some things and we, too, will say, "That's what we've been saying God was going to do! Praise God!"

Meanwhile, only worship and giving God the glory will keep our eyes on the invisible things of the spirit until faith becomes sight! When sight comes, it will be more real than the greatest natural reality you are currently facing. Great rejoicing comes when the baby is born.

When your family and friends are saved, healed, and delivered, it will wash away all the mountains of evidence that the enemy formerly held against them. The mountain of the past will be leveled and a stronghold of righteousness will form in their lives—and your eyes will behold it! Give God the glory for what He is doing now, before you can see it. Don't speak defeat, doubt words that give recognition to the evidence of failure, loss, and pain.

Release faith words in worship and watch what happens.

Key 8

Fully Persuaded

"And being fully persuaded that, what he had promised, he was able also to perform."

ROMANS 4:21

It is one thing to believe that God gave us a promise, but it is another thing to believe (be fully persuaded) that He is going to do it.

It's one thing to believe with a half-hearted assent to the fulfillment of the promise, and another to step into the full measure of faith that defeats all other persuasions.

Being fully persuaded at the promise and performance of it means, "I am totally convinced, through and through, without any doubt, nothing wavering, from the top of my head to the soles of my feet, mind, body, and spirit, that the promise God has given me is true—so true that I have no shadow of a doubt that God is going to fully perform exactly what He said."

God has promised many things in His Word, including salvation, healing, and deliverance. We have to be fully persuaded that

He is able to save, heal, and deliver our families, our cities, and those who are closest to us. When you look at your unsaved children, don't consider the mountain. Instead, speak God's Word and make it the reality. Begin to prophesy the Word of God.

He has released the *rhema* word of prophecy to us, revealing our specific role as a people in His plan. He's given us our role, our identity, and our assignment through prophetic words. In other words, He has told us our Sarah is going to bear a baby in spite of her dead womb.

Abraham's part and our part are all a piece of God's history with His people on earth. He has always had a people He has chosen and used for the unveiling of His ultimate plan for earth and humanity. Here we are, centuries after Abraham, and God has chosen us and shown us that He wants to use us as believers to do that which is too hard, too big, too impossible, and so far out of our reach that only He can do it through us.

I would never want to paint a picture of Abraham as never having had a bad day on his faith journey. He was as human as we are. The point is that he did not make a habit of unbelief, and if he fell, he got back up and kept traveling the path God called him to walk. He had to battle his mind at times, just like you and I do, but he overcame it through his devotional life and personal relationship with God.

I believe there is a level of faith working in the revival and harvest field of the church today. There are people who have stepped into God's "promise field" and are walking, just walking and believing.

Some people actually think they are doing nothing because all they are doing is walking and believing God for what He promised. They know they can't make it happen, so they walk, looking neither to right or the left, even though they are accused of being unproductive for the Kingdom of God.

It takes a deep kind of faith to do what no one else is doing, to break with the old patterns of reproduction. The church has programmed reproduction to death, giving seminars, teaching a hundred classes on witnessing, and holding sessions on equipping the church with the latest and best methods of "becoming pregnant with the harvest."

Abraham and Sarah learned the hard way that you cannot "get yourself pregnant and give birth to God's destiny child" by an alternate plan of man's making. Our methods today of building the church may be somewhat void of God's plan because we tend to rely on what we can make happen, what pleases our senses, and what settles our minds.

A powerful, prophetic move of God is under way today towards His church. He is after the "dead womb of the church" so that He can bring about a "son of destiny" that will touch the nations of the world. Only a true move of God can fill that womb. It is imperative that we do not try to fill it just because it appears that God is not. That is a disaster waiting to happen.

Disciples are made while obeying God's Word. The church has a great mandate on it to win the lost, to evangelize the world, but it is going to take disciples to do it, those who have learned obedience at the sound of God's voice.

We exhibit our faith when we believe and obey God. We prove our faith when we refuse to step into any alternate self-help plans that will "help along the plan of God." There are people today who are set on maturing in their faith so that the wavering and unbelief will be the minority voice instead of the majority.

When God has given us a Word, whether for revival in our

church and city, healing for our bodies, or salvation for our families, we have to step into the invisible world of faith and believe that God is going to do what we cannot currently see with our natural eyes, think with our minds, or have the talent or skill to bring about. God's Word, in written and *rhema* voice, is more sure and concrete than anything on earth.

One thing repeated in the Scriptures is the one sense that God expects us to use: our ears.

"He that hath ears to hear, let him hear" (Matthew 11:15).

"He that hath an ear, let him hear what the Spirit saith unto the churches" (Revelation 2:7).

We have heard; let us believe!

epilogue

The Final Chapter Has Not Yet Been Written...
Impossible Plans in Impossible Places

> "With men this is impossible;
> but with God all things are possible."
> MATTHEW 19:26

Hudson Taylor said this: "I have found that there are three stages in every great work of God: first, it is impossible, then it is difficult, then it is done."

People of historic numbers have been brought to the brink of seemingly insane proposals by God—not because they were seeking them, but because God interrupted them. If they had been looking for something to do, this would not have been it.

I have two questions for you:

Has God placed you in an impossible place?

Do you have a set of impossible plans that have been delivered to you?

Some of you who are reading this know this is about you because the Lord appeared to you in some fashion and called you out to a place that others would not understand.

It appears that over and over, when no one is really seeking God for these kinds of calls, He suddenly appears, interrupting the flow of life to set people on a path that requires more of them than they ever think they can give.

I do not believe God chooses people who will tell Him "no," though they may have to have His plans spelled out for them.

He chooses people He knows and has confidence in, those who have a heart to say "yes."

He knows something about them that they do not even know about themselves.

He knows what they are made of, and has chosen them because they have what it takes to follow through in obedience to the "finish."

Quite a few years ago, my husband and I were in an especially trying place in our ministry. I was talking to my father on the phone, telling him I was ready to give up on the ministry because of people. He told me, "Esther, you were raised for this. You have it in you. You have it in you to stand in these places. You were born and equipped for the ministry!" His words gave me an insight into the training fields of God. Some of them are very unlikely, but basic, trainings.

Many people who were ready and willing to obey God have said "yes" to Him without being aware of how much it would cost along the way.

They have been ordinary people just like you and me.

Abraham was living in an idolatrous country (he was asked to take a walk on an undisclosed path and later asked to sacrifice his son; see Genesis 12:1 and 22:2). This father of a nation stepped with faith into totally unknown territories, trusting God to the ultimate with his family, life, and future. He was asked to go without a road map to a place only God knew. He was later asked to offer his only son, Isaac, to the Lord.

We really have to work to move ourselves into Abraham's life, to understand it as more than a nice Bible story that illustrates faith. When it is our turn, and God is asking us to step out to walk in His not-so-clear-path, this is when we begin to understand the cost of following the Lord at this level. It has moved us from normal faith into a realm that stretches us beyond ourselves.

When this walk actually begins to hurt our normal-thinking brain and nothing computes anymore, we know we have reached a true path of faith-walking, where we will walk by faith and not by sight.

Moses was living it up in Pharaoh's palace (called to deliver his people; see Exodus 3:4–10). He had it all, but one day a burning recognition that he was not destined to remain in Pharaoh's palace brought him to a place of decision.

One may have a great ministry, a good church, and a nice home and family setting to live out life comfortably, but when God appears and begins to burn a call into the heart of a man or woman, all former comfort zones are challenged and removed.

While it may appear hard, senseless, or crazy to others, once the call to move out comes and the decision is made, somehow the willingness to pay the price is birthed in the human spirit. The things that once surrounded our lives suddenly become insignificant. This is what accounts for multitudes of people through the centuries who have left it all behind to go where God called them.

Sometimes it is not a physical move that is made, as in Moses and Abraham's case, but a move in the heart that totally transitions the path we were on. Many leaders have remained in the same town, city, or nation, but found that for all intents and purposes, they had left it all behind to follow the Lord. Many pastors, evangelists, prophets, missionaries, apostles, and teachers have done this—stayed in their places of ministry but changed paths. This has, for many, brought just as much reproach among their families and friends as if they had sold all their goods and moved to outer space!

It makes no sense to others when you depart from what everyone considers conventional. So, staying or leaving, there are those who are on a journey that many will not understand.

Noah was trying to raise his family in a godless society (called to build an ark of safety; see Genesis 6:13–14). He stood out like a sore thumb to his whole society. He was mocked by everyone who passed by his "dream boat." His call was to build something no one would understand. It made no sense to a single soul. It appeared to be a huge monstrosity right in the middle of everyone's neighborhood.

He and his world were diametrically opposed.

This is what the move of God looks like to a religious world. It appears to be outrageous, insane, and bothersome to the rest of the world. The bitterness and anger against such a movement can build to a raging crescendo. There are people today who refute what God's chosen men and women have done in "building an ark" for a society that is ready to drown in its own degradation. The ark is a constant rebuke to their way of life.

I wonder what religion looked like in Noah's day. Did it look somewhat like what is developing today as a great mixture of religious thoughts and tolerance have invaded the world (including the church), which in turn makes today's Noahs look intolerant because we still decry sin and call for a return to holiness?

God has raised up ministers of the gospel all over the world to place an "ark of safety" in the midst of a dying world, but the price is to be paid for those who dare to be so bold.

Joseph was dreaming and living as a favored son in his father's house (from prison to reigning; see Genesis 37:28 and 41:41). It's a hard row to hoe when your brothers do not believe in God's call upon your life. You stepped out of the boat and they don't like it. There are those today who have been ostracized by their denominations for stepping beyond the boundaries that traditional religion sets for them. Some have been dismissed. Others have been thrown into pits and called dead. But in truth, all of this is part of God's plan for them.

It takes a radical believer of God's call to endure the pain of rejection from those you trusted the most. Some revivalists, pastors, and evangelists alike have endured the loss of fellowship with friends and the loss of members of their churches. They have been met with closed doors that once welcomed them—all because of the "dream," all because of the "vision." Many national pastors in third-world countries have been threatened with death, beatings, and prison. They have been called out of idolatry to serve the Living God and called out to believe in Jesus Christ rather than the gods of their nations. And for this, they have paid dearly at the hands of their former friends and families.

For Joseph, it was all about "training for reigning." For some of you in a "pit" right now, it is about the same thing. God never loses His place or forgets where you are. And it is all for a purpose...

Joseph's was a very difficult path, but it led to a place where he was able to impact a nation that formerly would have been hostile to him. He was put in place by God as a type of "salvation" for his people in time of drought. His brothers who had thrown him away and then sold him as chattel property came to where he was placed by God to seek help from him.

Gideon hid behind the winepress in a time of oppression (called to lead the battle against the enemy; see Judges 6:11–12).

> And there came an angel of the Lord, and sat under an oak which was in Ophrah, that pertained unto Joash the Abiezrite: and his son Gideon threshed wheat by the winepress, to hide it from the Midianites. And the angel of the Lord appeared unto him, and said unto him, "The Lord is with thee, thou mighty man of valor."

Gideon was chosen to lead a battle that he formerly had been hiding from. He had managed to carry wheat into an unlikely place to hide from the enemy—by the wine press. Maybe he thought that the enemy would always look in the obvious place: the threshing floor for wheat, but not by the wine press. He was pretty clever in what He did, but it still was defensive by nature. God wanted Gideon to move on the offensive against the enemy so he and his kinsmen would no longer have to hide the goods from those who were consistently stealing from them.

A few years ago, a man entered our Wednesday night prayer meeting. I felt he had something for our church from the Holy Spirit and asked him if God had given him something. He spoke with spiritual wisdom and knowledge concerning our placement, but the most memorable thing he said was, "The devil has no choice but to stop you."

This is how it was and is with Israel and her enemies, and this is how it is with the people of God and His church. A satanic

DNA is infused into the hearts of those who scheme to stop God's people, to destroy, to steal, and to kill.

Some of you have been chosen to stand in a place where you have faced tremendous darkness, both satanic and human. The ground around you is hard and hostile. You have taken a lot of harassment from men and devils just because of who you are and where you are. The enemy has been stealing from you, your family, your city, and your church…and maybe you find yourself repeatedly in a defensive mode.

But God has entrusted this hard and hostile ground to YOU. Yes, it's hard ground, but anyone God has chosen, regardless of his or her natural strength or gifts, is not only entrusted with the task, but is totally capable of working the ground God has given. God chooses the most unlikely people to do things no one else would have ever picked them for. God saw something in Gideon that he would have never identified in himself. God called him a "mighty man of valor."

Gideon, through obedience, rose up and went into battle with the diminished army God chose for him. Even the numbers game many people play is not enough to win what God will win through a man like Gideon who believes God in a tough time of warfare.

Jesus' disciples were mending their nets and fishing, working like ordinary men of their day, when Jesus interrupted their world. He set them in a place that was incredibly difficult: to face their church, their friends, their family, their culture, their cities, their long-standing, religiously solid Temple and preach that the Messiah was Jesus when very few desired to believe it.

The disciples were called by God to do something so out of character, outrageous, and extraordinary within their religious world and its traditions that a "yes" would immediately place them in the middle of great controversy and conflict. For many, it would bring them to the brink of disaster and persecution like they had never known. They would face ridicule, threats, and ostracism. They would face hard choices in which their integrity would be tested. But God believed in them!

They were asked to risk it all for the cause of Christ and take a step apart from others' norms to do it. We tend to immortalize these people because their names are in the Bible, but they were all mortal men and women in the grip of God.

God has always found Himself a man or woman, set up His burning bush, sanctified the ground, commissioned the person/people, and has given the vision, mandate, and the authority of the rod. Only with impossible plans in impossible places can man exhibit faith and God show His power. "It's not by might or power, but by MY SPIRIT, says the Lord" (Zechariah 4:6).

God has never asked anyone to do anything easy. Even obedience to what He asks of people extracts a great personal cost. When He told His disciples to pick up their cross and follow Him, He knew what that was going to mean for them. To follow Him meant they would automatically be at odds with the world around them, both politically and religiously.

We can see the same dynamics today as we continue the long lineage of Christ until He comes again. We live in a season when God once again has escalated a move towards earth, which always indicates serious transition is taking place. God has continued to ask people to do some pretty incredible things! He has continued to place much confidence in mankind, choosing people who will stand firm and who are convinced, even in the face of fierce opposition and great difficulty.

Back to the two questions I asked at the beginning of this message:

Has God placed you in an impossible place?

Has a set of impossible plans been delivered to you?

Rest assured: God knows exactly what He's done, is doing, and will do in choosing you to stand for His cause. Impossible is just where God wants us because "With men this is impossible; but with God all things are possible" (Matthew 19:26).

You've joined the ranks of people all over the world who are still faithful today...nation to nation, praying, preaching, believing in God, and believing what He has called them to do! Praise God for the entrustment, no matter how difficult it may appear to you, for when it is done, God is going to be greatly glorified!

May God bless the impossible plans you hold in your heart!

Decree—Speak to Your Mountain!

Mountain, I see you and I know you! (1 Peter 5:8). I know my God is higher! (Psalms 61:2). I know you are smaller! Regardless of your appearance, you are never big enough to eclipse God with your shadow.

You may cast your shadow on mankind, but never on God and not on a servant of the Highest God! I reside under the shadow of the wings of God (Psalms 91:1) and refuse your shadow, which is nothing more than the shadow of death (Matthew 4:16).

You are despair, defeat, destruction, and death (John 10:10), but I am of a Kingdom of hope, victory, restoration, and life! I carry a mandate for your despair, your defeat, your destruction, and your death—but to me and mine, I declare life and liberty from your shadow!

I am not seated at your base, overshadowed by you. I have rejected your invitation to come to the top of your mountain. I have "come up higher," at the invitation of my God, to His mountain! I am seated with Christ, who is seated far above you, all your kingdoms, and all offers of compromise (Ephesians 2:6).

Because of your enormous size, I am made aware of how great God is because the Word declares I can cast you into the sea (Matthew 17:20; 21:21 and Mark 11:23) and you have to go! That is the power of one servant of God, the God whose throne inhabits eternity (Isaiah 57:15).

The ageless One saw you formed. He knows what you are made of, and you are but dust in His sight. With a single breath of His nostrils, He blows you into oblivion (Exodus 15:6–8).

And because I have God's breath in me, I can breathe, prophesy, and decree—and it is as I have decreed. Your end, your demise, your fall, and your ruin are as sure as the Word of God that is breathed from my mouth as a servant of the Highest God!

About the Author

Esther Seaton Dummer is the daughter of pioneer pastors, Delbert and Mary Seaton, who have cut deep furrows in the fields of their labor for their Lord and Master. Now Esther and her husband of more than forty-two years, Loren, have the plow in their hands and follow the generational blessing of ministry to God's people.

God has blessed the Dummers with three grown, married children: Donna, Debra, and Daniel, and fourteen grandchildren who are the delight of their hearts.

Esther and Loren Dummer have had the privilege of pastoring some of God's finest disciples at Gateway Worship Center in Clatskanie, Oregon, where they have served for eighteen years. While they have faced challenges of all magnitudes, God has been faithful to carry them through the storms, the fires, and the floods of adversity. His blessings have been evident over and over as the Dummers have pursued their vision and promise with their congregation.

Esther Dummer, who finished this book on her sixty-second birthday, February 14, 2010, has been writing for many years. This is her first published book; however, many are familiar with her message through the ministry message called "CheckPoint" she has written for about twelve years.

With a deep love for God's Word and the integrity of the same, she has been teaching for the better part of her life, writing her own curriculum, a series similar to this book that challenges the student of the Word to get up and grow. In releasing this book, she says, "My desire is to see a greater readership that can be blessed by what God has given me. I consider myself a servant of God who is simply doing what He has called me to do—write."

She also founded and leads a ministry called Going Up to High Places, an outreach of Gateway that gathers twice a year to provide a place where pastors and other Christian leaders and intercessors can come for a time of teaching and refreshing.